P9-CCT-832

Flow in Sports

Susan A. Jackson, PhD
Queensland University of Technology

Mihaly Csikszentmihalyi, PhD
Claremont Graduate University

Human Kinetics

Library of Congress Cataloging-in-Publication Data

Jackson, Susan A., 1963–
    Flow in sports / Susan A. Jackson, Mihaly Csikszentmihalyi.
      p. cm.
    Includes bibliographical reference (p.) and index.
    ISBN 0-88011-876-8
      1. Sports--Psychological aspects.   2. Athletes--Psychology.
    3. Happiness.   I. Csikszentmihalyi, Mihaly.   II. Title.
    796'.01--dc21   99-12526
                                                                 CIP

ISBN-10: 0-88011-876-8
ISBN-13- 978-0-88011-876-7

Developmental Editor: Anne Mischakoff Heiles; **Assistant Editor:** Laurie Stokoe; **Copyeditor:** Anne Mischakoff Heiles; **Proofreader:** Sarah Wiseman; **Indexer:** Gerry Lynn Messner; **Graphic Designer:** Robert Reuther; **Graphic Artist:** Roberta Edwards; **Photo Editors:** Amy Parker and Clark Brooks; **Cover Designer:** Jack Davis; **Photographer (cover):** © Agence Vahdystadt/Richard Martin; **Printer:** Total Printing Systems

Human Kinetics books are available at special discounts for bulk purchase. Special editions or book excerpts can also be created to specification. For details, contact the Special Sales Manager at Human Kinetics.

Printed in the United States of America   20 19 18 17 16 15

The paper in this book is certified under a sustainable forestry program.

Human Kinetics
Website: www.HumanKinetics.com

United States: Human Kinetics
P.O. Box 5076
Champaign, IL 61825-5076
800-747-4457
e-mail: info@hkusa.com

Canada: Human Kinetics
475 Devonshire Road, Unit 100
Windsor, ON N8Y 2L5
800-465-7301 (in Canada only)
e-mail: info@hkcanada.com

Europe: Human Kinetics
107 Bradford Road
Stanningley
Leeds LS28 6AT, United Kingdom
+44 (0)113 255 5665
e-mail: hk@hkeurope.com

For information about Human Kinetics' coverage in other areas of the world, please visit our website: www.HumanKinetics.com

To Stephan and Jack

—Susan A. Jackson

contents

PART I   Understanding Flow   1

PART II   Experiencing Flow   33

preface

To feel completely at one with what you are doing, to know you are strong and able to control your destiny at least for the moment, and to gain a sense of pleasure independent of results is to experience flow. The flow state has many names—optimal experience, playing in the zone, feeling on a high, and being totally focused are some of the more common labels. Whatever words you use to describe flow experiences, they're sure to be associated with the most precious moments in your memory.

Sport offers plentiful opportunities to experience flow. Yet the flow state eludes most athletes and seems mysterious and unachievable to many coaches. Indeed, most athletes experience flow by chance. And little wonder, because the conditions most conducive to experiencing flow and its components have not been adequately explained to athletes and coaches. Their options were to wait for flow or try to force it to occur, but this rarely leads to the desired outcome.

We have written *Flow in Sports* to increase the understanding and incidence of the flow experience in sport. This is not a "12-steps-to-flow" book. Flow would be a simpler but shallower phenomenon if access to it were so easy. On the contrary, finding flow involves a keen awareness and a grasp of a set of factors that combine to set the stage for it. Underlying the flow experience are sharp mental skills. We will give you information to understand and apply the flow components to your specific situation.

In the chapters that follow, we hope to make flow a more familiar, yet no less exciting, phenomenon, one that you can experience and use for your own purposes—yet never fully control on command. We will explain each key component of flow and, through examples and reports of interviews with athletes, demonstrate its relevance. After reading this book you will understand and recognize flow better, and through effective application of important principles you will be in a position to more consistently experience flow in your sport, as well as in other lifetime activities.

While this is a collaborative authorship by the two of us, you might make more sense of the material if we explain our respective roles. As the world's foremost expert on flow, Dr. Csikszentmihalyi (pronounced "CHICK-sent-me-high-ee") brought to the project a wealth of knowledge and research material on the topic. He helped identify the key subject areas to be addressed and established the framework for the book through his many years of research. Throughout the development of the manuscript he provided invaluable insights from his understanding of the flow state. Dr. Jackson was the driving force who brought this much-needed work to reality. Her studies and interviews with athletes specifically about flow set her on a mission to write the book you are about to read. A sabbatical spent on a visit to the University of Chicago, where she consulted with her coauthor, confirmed her commitment to the project. Dr. Jackson conducted most of the interviews from which material is quoted in this book. We have interspersed quotations from well-known figures that seem appropriate; these materials come from a variety of popular print sources, including newspapers and sport periodicals.

We would not suggest that this is the final, definitive work on the subject of flow in sport. Like us, many writers and researchers have delved into this intriguing area of study, and we have brought related and relevant work to your attention in the notes section at the end of the book.

Whether you are an athlete who is seeking to maximize your sport performance and experience, a coach looking to expand your methods of and knowledge for mentoring your players, or a student of sport adding to your information base in this important area of study, we hope that the reading experience and results from it will be well worth your time.

acknowledgments

Writing this book has been a long-standing goal that would not have been possible without the support and assistance of numerous people at various stages from its conception to final production. My gratitude is first extended to Mihaly Csikszentmihalyi, with whom I have the honor of coauthoring this book. Having the opportunity to share the writing of my first book with a best-selling author and the foremost authority on flow has indeed been a special privilege.

I have also been fortunate to know as mentors and friends Dan Gould, Jay Kimiecik, Herb Marsh, Ken Ravizza, and Tara Scanlan, each of whom has provided support and assistance to me as I have developed my work in the area of flow. There have been many others from the field of sport psychology who have provided encouragement, collaboration, or feedback. In particular, I would like to acknowledge Steve Ford, Doug Newburg, Glyn Roberts, Gary Stein, and Pat Thomas for their contributions to research studies on flow in sport. Time spent at the University of Chicago allowed me to interact with a number of flow scholars, and I would especially like to thank Antonella Delle Fave (University of Milan), Jeanne Nakamura, John Patton, and Jennifer Schmidt for much appreciated conversations and collaborations.

To the athletes and coaches who have participated in studies on flow, and to the many friends I have made through sport who have helped me to experience and witness flow in action, thank you for the insights.

Rainer Martens, by responding enthusiastically to the idea for this book, and providing continued support as it began to take shape, has enabled the project to come to fruition. All the team at Human Kinetics who have been involved with the book at its various stages have been energetic in their assistance. Special thanks to Anne Heiles for her enthusiastic support and attention to detail and to Laurie Stokoe for her conscientious help.

To my husband Stephan, thank you for endless patience, encouragement, and support during the challenging times in which this book was written; and to our son Jack, you are my source of joy and inspiration.

—Susan A. Jackson

Understanding
Flow

PART I

1

Being in Flow

If you stop to think about it, you'll probably agree that when we leave it up to chance, life can be rather unpleasant. Much of what we do in a lifetime is stressful, from the days of dreading the teacher's call to the blackboard to the years of worrying about our job, family, or health. Even though life these days is much safer and more comfortable on average than at any time else in history, dangers and discomforts are never very far away. And when we are not stressed or anxious, we are likely to feel bored sitting in a stifling classroom, office, or apartment.

Yet the value of our lives depends largely on how we feel toward our experiences as we move from birth to old age. Some of us will waste the only opportunity we have to experience life as it can be—a wonderfully enjoyable, stimulating, satisfying state of being—because year after year we feel stressed and bored.

Yet in actuality life offers great richness, and it certainly is not all stressful or boring. There are moments that stand out from the chaos of the everyday as shining beacons. In many ways, one might say that the whole effort of humankind through millennia of history has been to capture these fleeting moments of fulfillment and make them more a part of everyday existence. Religious rituals, works of art, and musical performances are some examples of how we have tried to replace "nature red of tooth and claw" by ordered practices that improve the quality of life.

One of these fruits of civilization is sport. From the earliest times, men and women have learned to use the body in ways that provide the greatest physical pleasure and mental enjoyment. And these athletic performances and events have been so intense that in many cultures they became the centerpieces of religious celebration. From the Olympic games of the ancient Greeks to the Mayan ball games, ordered athletic competition served as a concrete demonstration of spirit over matter, of the divine essence potentially present in the physical body.

Much has changed since those times, and now most people are attracted to sport for more practical reasons: they hope to keep their weight or blood pressure down, want to excel over the competition, or dream of making a great deal of money in the professional leagues. But whatever other reasons motivate the athlete, the crux of sport is the *quality of experience* it provides. Contrary to what happens in most of life, sport can offer a state of being that is so rewarding one does it for no other reason than to be a part of it. Here is how a swimmer we interviewed described this kind of experience:

> When I've been happiest with my performance, I've sort of felt one with the water and my stroke and everything. . . . I was really tuned into what I was doing. I knew exactly how I was going to swim the race, and I just knew I had it all under control, and I got in and I was really aware of what everyone in the race was doing. . . . I was just totally absorbed in my stroke, and I knew I was passing them but I didn't care. I mean it's not that I didn't care; I was going, "Oh, this is cool!" And I just swam and won, and I was totally in control of the situation. It felt really cool.

A runner offered a similar description:

> I felt really in control, just felt terrific the whole way, and didn't feel the pain that I would normally feel in that run. . . . [I] just really enjoyed the experience of running and really had probably the most successful race ever of my life. . . . It wasn't as painful as the others. I felt very in control, I felt very strong. I was able to run as I had planned. . . . I felt really focused. I just felt like, you know, like athletes say, "It clicked"; it felt great the whole way.

Athletes in all sports, all over the world, seek moments like these. The feelings involved are among the most intense, most memorable experiences one can get in this life. The state they describe is what we call *flow*, or optimal experience. Once attained, flow experiences remain etched in the memory and provide the blueprint for returning to this optimal state. Yet experiencing flow is not easy. This book will explain how flow experiences are achieved in sport and identify conditions that make it more likely to occur.

© Claus Andersen

DEFINING FLOW

The accounts the two athletes, the swimmer and runner, gave describe several components of the flow experience. First of all, it is a state of consciousness where one becomes totally absorbed in what one is doing, to the exclusion of all other thoughts and emotions. So flow is about focus. More than just focus, however, flow is a harmonious experience where mind and body are working together effortlessly, leaving the person feeling that something special has just occurred. So flow is also about enjoyment. People associate flow with peak performance, as the swimmer's and runner's comments show. Although winning is important, flow does not depend on it, and flow offers something more than just a successful outcome. This is because flow lifts experience from the ordinary to the optimal, and it is in those moments that we feel truly alive and in tune with what we are doing.

Flow is a state with universal qualities that is experienced by people in a wide range of contexts. Elderly German gardeners describe the feeling of intense involvement they experience when tending their roses with similar words as Japanese teenagers use to describe how it feels to race their motorcycles. Navajo shepherds following their flocks on horseback also mention similar experiences, which sound much like those reported by Hindu mystics—or by dedicated athletes all over the world.

Among all the things that people do in their lives, sport presents a special opportunity for flow to occur. There are few activities—such as performing music, or drama, or playing chess—that are as apt to make flow happen. But even though the sport setting is structured to enhance flow, many athletes have trouble achieving it. While we cannot guarantee that reading this book will make more frequent flow experiences happen, we can shed light on the forces within and outside a person that make the experience of flow more likely to occur. We can help you analyze what especially turns flow on for you and how you experience this optimal state. We can tell you how others have discovered flow, and you can pick out from their experiences what may help you understand and maximize optimal experiences during your sport participation.

By studying the quality of experience people have had with flow in many different activities, Csikszentmihalyi and colleagues have shown that sport in particular is associated with a number of very positive qualities. Figure 1.1, which reports on a sample of adolescents, compares sport with academic school work and watching TV. The vertical axis represents the Experience Sampling Method (ESM) responses, or the scores for each of the variables on the horizontal axis; these scores are obtained by asking people at several randomly chosen times each day how they feel while they are doing various activities.

THE CHALLENGE-SKILLS BALANCE AND FLOW

A first requisite for flow is striking a positive balance between these two elements: the challenges you think you face and the skills you think you have. This is a simple but important concept that we will refer to throughout the book as the *CS balance*, and it is critical to understanding how flow occurs. *C* stands for challenges, and *S* for skills.

The CS balance is a golden rule of flow. Later in the book we present more specific information about how you can change the balance of challenges and skills to increase the chances of flow occurring.

One point to remember here is that it is your subjective perception that predicts flow. This means that is it not so much what the objective challenges or skills are in a situation that determines the quality of experience, but what a person *thinks* of the available opportunities and of her capacity to act. So whether you are in flow in sport or

(margin handwriting: CS Balance → Challeng/skills balance)

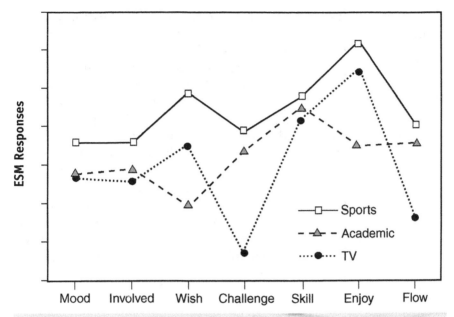

Figure 1.1 ESM responses from a sample of more than 800 representative U.S. adolescents aged 11 to 18. Source: Unpublished data from the Sloan Study of Adolescent Development (1995), C. Bidwell, M. Csikszentmihalyi, L. Hedges, and B. Schneider, principal investigators. The University of Chicago.

whether you suffer from anxiety or boredom depends to a large extent on your perception.

Both challenges and skills can be progressively developed in clearly defined stages of increasing complexity. The further one moves up the skill dimension in sport, the more difficult the challenges become. Breaking the four-minute mile was seen—in its day—as the ultimate challenge: many elite, middle-distance runners took up this challenge, trying to stretch the boundaries of human performance in this domain. Once the four-minute mile was achieved, new challenges were set; today's elite distance runners have times of their own making that set the outer limit of potential achievement.

Let's turn briefly to see how the CS balance sets the stage for flow. Think of a situation in sport in which you felt you could meet the challenge. Maybe it was an important competition that you trained hard for. As you lined up for the start of the competition, you felt eager and a little nervous: eager because you were well-prepared, nervous because this competition meant a lot, and you would have to give it your best shot. You believed you could meet the challenge, but because the situation was not an easy one, you needed to apply all the effort you were capable of.

The best athletes thrive in such situations. They know what to do and believe they can succeed. There is order in their consciousness, with clear goals focusing their thoughts so intensely that not enough attention is left over to even worry about themselves or their problems. Concentration is directed totally toward the activity. The players are so in tune with what they are doing that they quickly notice the finest nuances of their game and make adjustments to stay in the groove.

This optimal state of flow comes about when a person's abilities match his or her opportunities for action—in other words, when the CS balance is operating. Now use the exercise that follows to see if you can recall other moments in your sport when you experienced the CS balance and remember in more detail how you felt during such moments.

Recalling Flow Experiences

The following exercise will help you to understand flow. Take a piece of paper and write down your response to the following:

Think of a time when you were totally involved in what you were doing— a time when you felt strong and positive, not worried about yourself or about failing. Describe the situation as fully as possible: when and where it occurred, who you were with, what was happening leading up to this time, and how the experience started. As you recall your experience, use as many senses as you can to imagine the event. Jot down thoughts, feelings, and impressions of the experience, including how you felt after it finished.

You may have experienced this type of involvement in an activity many times or only once. Your experience may have occurred at work, during sport, or while having a good time with friends. Some people experience flow often; others rarely, if at all. The fact is that anyone who can focus his or her attention can experience flow. The better you can recall what was happening before and during a moment when you experienced flow, the easier it will be to set the stage for it to happen again.

HOW A CYCLIST DESCRIBES FLOW

Oftentimes we can connect with flow by hearing how others describe their optimal experiences. We introduce here Simon, an elite cyclist whose description of a flow experience follows. In the following chapter, where each of the dimensions of flow are described, we again refer to examples provided by Simon regarding his optimal experiences. You will find examples from Simon interspersed throughout the book.

> It was the final day of the Tour. Wearing the yellow jersey, I had 100 kilometers to go to defend it to the finish. The end of the 100k was a 7k climb, and I was amongst internationals with a higher climbing stature than myself. There was a lot of pressure there, but a lot of prestige to uplift it, and I pulled it off. I was totally absorbed, 110 percent; that was all that mattered in the whole existence. It just amazed me how I could maintain such high concentration for three hours. I'm used to having my mind wander, especially under pressure. My body felt great. Nothing, you feel like just nothing can go wrong and there's nothing that will be able to stop you or get in your way. And you're ready to tackle anything, and you don't fear any possibility happening, and it's just exhilarating. Afterward, I couldn't come down, I was on a high. I felt like I wanted to go ride, ride up that hill again.

Experiences like the one Simon describes are very special flow moments, the type of experience that remains etched in the athlete's memory. Not all flow experiences will be so exhilarating, but all are rewarding. Knowing what cues lead to flow can help you get the most enjoyment out of sport and physical activity. In this book, we will discuss factors that athletes have found useful in this respect. However, *you* are probably your most important source of information about flow experiences. That is, the crucial source is the one that resides within each of us as individuals, because it is the particular way a person uses information that determines the experiences he or she has. Therefore, the clearer an idea you have of what makes flow possible for you, the better your chances of replicating the experience again and again.

In our research, it has been amazing to discover how consistently athletes describe their feelings at these peak moments. Some quotes may trigger an "aha" experience for you, helping you recall similar moments in your own sport participation:

> I feel as if I'm very involved in the event, but my involvement is without a huge input on my part. It's almost as if I'm floating from one place to another . . . purely through instinct more than anything else.

Well, you don't feel pain. You don't feel like you're going too hard or too softly; you just flow. Just flowing, you can't feel yourself breathe—it's not a laboring. It's really efficient—you feel like you're being really efficient. And you feel like you're a motor: you are a machine. But you're controlling your machine. It's like being in a state of suspension—you judge the correct pace for your fitness level, sort of psychic.

You can see why this optimal experience came to be known as flow. The athlete in the second quote referred to flow and flowing in her description of what was happening when she was in this special state. Mihaly Csikszentmihalyi, when first investigating states of total involvement among a wide range of people and activities, found his respondents used the term *flow* in their descriptions. The term captures the essence of what happens when one becomes totally absorbed in an activity.

Common themes have been found in descriptions of total involvement that lead to optimal experience. Indeed, flow seems to have a set of universal characteristics, which we describe in detail in the next chapter. We will conclude this chapter by trying to put the flow concept into the context of other terms that have been used in association with optimal moments.

EXPRESSIONS ATHLETES USE TO DESCRIBE THE FLOW STATE

Many terms have been used to describe those moments when things are going really well in sport: "in the groove," "on a high," "on auto," or "in the zone," to name a few. Table 1.1 lists some expressions athletes commonly use to describe being in flow. You probably have your own ways of describing optimal moments and could add these to the list in Table 1.1.

Flow was first described as an ("autotelic") experience, to denote a state of mind that was intrinsically rewarding. The word *autotelic* is derived from two Greek words that describe doing something for its own sake (*auto* = self; *telos* = goal). Flow is a simpler term, and one that people often use in describing these types of experiences.

When people talk about their flow experiences, they mention two key characteristics: that these special times are enjoyable and optimal. For this reason the terms *enjoyment* and *optimal experience* will be used interchangeably with flow throughout this book. You can think of enjoyment and optimal experience as two points along a continuum. Enjoyment may be more descriptive of the lower to middle levels of flow, while optimal experience denotes the higher levels.

To distinguish flow from similar concepts, *peak performance* will be used to describe one's highest level of performance. Athletes usually experience flow during peak performance, but it is not necessarily the case that peak performance will follow every flow experience.

Another term that shares many similarities with flow is *peak experience*. As originally coined by the psychologist Abraham Maslow, peak experience refers to moments of highest happiness that may or may not be of our own doing. These may also have the characteristics of flow, but flow is not reserved only for these extraordinary moments. Flow can occur during simple activities, like playing throw-and-catch with a friend. This is probably not a defining event in anyone's life,

Table 1.1	
Expressions Athletes Use to Describe the Flow State	
In the bubble	Going really well
Complete satisfaction	Nothing else matters
Focused	Weightlessness
In the zone	In the groove
Total involvement	Optimal pace
Peaceful	Flowing
On auto	Tuned in
Everything clicks	Easy speed
Switched on	In control
Tough and not puff	Strong
Concentration	Total composure and confidence
Going fast and doing it easily	Floating
Ideal	Super alive
Unbeatable	Total control

Your own terms for describing flow:

but it can be an enjoyable experience, lifting the spirits momentarily. Sport flow also occurs, of course, at the upper ends of the continuum, where peak and optimal experience merge. These are the moments that athletes remember and treasure, and because they are so clearly above the ordinary, they are often the first to be recalled when athletes describe times they have been in flow.

WHY FLOW IS IMPORTANT FOR ATHLETES

Achieving peak performance is an all-important goal for competitive athletes and coaches, and flow can facilitate such outcomes. The mindset accompanying flow tends to push a person to his or her limits, and this is one reason why flow is so important to athletes seeking to do their best. As athletes and coaches know all too well, it is difficult to have the body perform to high levels when the mind is not focused.

While flow is important for those seeking peak performance, flow experiences are also rewarding for their own sake, regardless of the outcomes they may produce. When too focused on outcomes, you can easily miss the experience. If you are so concerned about winning an event, you may miss the mental state that is likely to help bring it about. This can be disastrous for performance. Even worse, if you miss the feeling of enjoyment that justifies the existence of sports in the first place, what have you really gained?

Thus, while an event that involves flow may also be defined as a peak experience or a peak performance, there are many other opportunities for flow that are not reserved for moments of highest happiness or best performance. Flow starts with simple absorbing moments at one end of the continuum and the defining moments of optimal experience at the other end. Both types of experience help make sport involvement worthwhile, and in this book we cover strategies that should help athletes and coaches find flow at various levels.

But flow is not only for those involved in sport professionally. It is true that many of the examples and ideas contained in the remainder of this book come from the authors' research with elite performers, and such athletes should find *Flow in Sports* helpful to their pursuit of excellence. However, the capacity to experience flow is not limited to being a high-level performer, and it certainly doesn't depend on professional status. The concept of CS balance holds for anyone; we all can find flow at an appropriate level of competence. Recreational and fitness-oriented participants, like elite performers, also seek the greatest mental rewards and optimal experiences for the effort they devote to physical activity.

In addition to the positive transformation of experience, flow is a path to achieve personal growth by developing greater *complexity*. Because flow is so enjoyable, we tend to seek out situations where we can experience it. This necessarily involves developing skills and taking on increasingly greater challenges. You will discover, if you haven't already, that the CS balance is not static. It constantly moves upward.

Challenge-Skills balance

Just to maintain flow in your sport means you must keep increasing your skills. Furthermore, in increasing the intensity of the feeling you are led to increasingly higher levels of athletic performance.

Understanding flow, however, offers more than the development of athletic potential. Once the keys to flow are understood, the opportunity to develop one's whole life according to flow principles begins to emerge. At that point, it becomes possible to transform the entirety of life from a stressful and chaotic chase into something resembling an enjoyable dance.

2

Flow
FundaMentals

Is the way you feel during an exhilirating sport event—a great game or swim, a fabulous downhill race—similar to how you feel when you are reading a gripping novel or playing a close game of chess? At first thought your answer might be a loud, "Of course not!" After all, in sport you push your body to its limits of speed, skill, and endurance, whereas more passive activities like reading or chess involve only mental effort, imagination, or reasoning. So you might conclude that the sport experience is unique to physical activities; it differs from other activities, even those that are also enjoyable and worth doing for their own sake.

Yet one of the unexpected results of our series of studies of people's optimal experiences has been that despite the enormous differences between the activities individuals were doing, when whatever they were doing was enjoyable, they described their state of mind, or consciousness, in similar terms. Artists and surgeons—or dancers and rock climbers—seemed to share a set of feelings when they were deeply involved in what they liked to do. Although the contexts might differ greatly, the experience of people totally involved in what they are doing is characterized by a common set of features. Surgeons performing a life-and-death operation, chess players working out their next moves, or climbers scaling a mountain peak all described a consistent set of feelings that we identify as the flow dimensions. In this chapter, we describe nine of these dimensions and illustrate them with interviews of elite athletes.

Notice that "FundaMentals" in the title of this chapter contains a capital M. This is to emphasize how important the mental factor is to finding flow in sport. Flow is a psychological state, and this book focuses on how one can achieve it through control of the mind—or attention. Of course, physical, technical, and contextual components of sport also play important parts, and, where they are relevant to the focus of this book, these aspects are also discussed. However, because it is the mind-set that opens the possibility for flow in many different sport situations, it is the fundaMental components of flow that we describe in detail.

The following nine fundamental dimensions or components best describe the mind-set in flow:

1. Challenge-skills balance
2. Action-awareness merging
3. Clear goals
4. Unambiguous feedback
5. Concentration on the task at hand
6. Sense of control
7. Loss of self-consciousness
8. Transformation of time
9. Autotelic experience

We will describe each of these dimensions and demonstrate how they are experienced in the sport context. Simon, the cyclist introduced in the previous chapter, will provide examples of each of the dimensions in cycling. Quotes from a variety of performers will further illustrate the flow mind-set in sport.

FLOW COMPONENT #1— CHALLENGE-SKILLS BALANCE

This dimension of flow (which you read about in chapter 1) is the golden rule of flow. How do athletes experience this challenge-skills (CS) balance? "Challenging, but able to meet the challenge" is how a rower describes the kind of situation where the opportunities to act are at the upper ends of one's reach. To experience flow, it is not enough for challenges to equal skills; both factors need to be extending the person, stretching them to new levels. Athletes often find themselves in challenging situations; indeed, sport is about putting the physical body to the test and making the test conditions progressively more difficult. Challenges in sport come in a variety of forms, including physical, mental, and technical ones. Different types of sport challenges are discussed in chapter 3.

Elite athletes are always competing against opponents who are only a shade better or a shade worse, forcing them to use all their skills to stay even. It is essential for these athletes to know that no matter how difficult the task will be, it still is doable. A World Cup rugby finalist said about his team's final game, "I guess it was the extreme challenge, but we didn't approach it as a major hurdle." This quote points to the second part of the CS balance: perceived skills.

Why didn't the team approach the World Cup final as a major hurdle? Because the players were well-prepared and believed in their ability to be successful, having demonstrated superlative skills on their way to the final. This Australian team went on to win the World Cup final in a classy display of rugby skills.

Few athletes will find the challenge-skills balance in a World Cup final. For most, this would present a situation where challenges far outweighed skills, and they would find themselves experiencing anxiety. But flow is not reserved for elite athletes only. Each person can find her own balance appropriate to her present skill potential, and thus set the stage for flow. Challenges can be defined in a personal way, and may be far different from the obvious demands provided by the structure of a sport event. For example, most sports are designed with the goal of outperforming opponents as the main challenge. However, this need not be foremost in the minds of all athletes taking part in competition. It is what the athlete chooses to define as the challenge that determines what skills are needed to match the perceived opportunity.

Skills are set to a range of limits for different individuals, that is, we all differ in our individual capacities in different areas. However, it is not the objective skills that become critical in the CS balance, but rather how one perceives one's skills in relation to the relevant challenges (see chapter 3). It is important to realize that what you *believe* you can do will determine your experience more than will your actual abilities. As a runner said in discussing important factors for getting into flow, "I think probably the most important thing is the feeling that I've got the ability to be in that situation."

In most sport situations it is more than likely that it is the challenges that are high, making the skill or confidence component critical. There is always potential to increase challenges, but raising confidence can take a bit more work. For elite athletes, the expectations to perform are oftentimes stressful because the demands are so great. Being able to convert the stressors into challenge becomes the key to flow, as described by racing cyclist Simon:

I think there's a certain point at which you can convert stressful situations to challenge—rather than stressful things—which is where the flow sort of triggers off and you go, and it is like nothing is going to get in the way.

To be able to change how you view a particular situation takes self-confidence. To develop that confidence it helps to think back on past successes rather than on failures. It helps to focus the mind on your present strengths, whatever they happen to be.

FLOW COMPONENT #2— ACTION-AWARENESS MERGING

When you feel at one with the movements you are making, you are experiencing the second flow dimension: the merging of action and awareness. Instead of the mind looking at the body from the outside, as it were, the mind and body fuse into one. These are the moments poet William B. Yeats refers to in this verse:

O body swayed to music,

O brightening glance,

How can we know the dancer

From the dance?

This oneness with movement does not require effort in flow. Indeed the feedback is processed by the mind spontaneously, like breathing or pumping the pedals, as part of one seamless process. And it is this process, of the body and mind performing at the limits of their capacity and yet doing so effortlessly, that eventually produces total absorption, or the merging of action and awareness. When this occurs, a person feels at one with his or her actions. Simon explains what happens when he feels as though he becomes one with his bike:

It doesn't seem like you're sitting on a bike. You feel altogether like it's just one piece of machinery working together . . . like you're part of this machine that you were born with, and it's how you move.

Different athletes describe this oneness in a variety of ways, depending on their specialty. Rowers explain that the oar becomes an extension of the arm; basketball players feel literally merged with or part of the team—as the arm feels part of the body—and when they shoot a basket, the arc of the ball toward the hoop is like an extension of their mind and will.

Action and awareness merge only when you become totally absorbed in what you are doing. This comes about when you feel that
you have the skills to meet the challenge and when you focus all your
attention on the task at hand. As with all the flow dimensions, action-
awareness merging is part of a holistic experience and dependent on
the other components. Athletes describe this total absorption in very
positive terms: "Everything feels very smooth and fluent," "[I'm] totally absorbed in my stroke," "[It's] in the groove." Some athletes focus on the fact that nothing else enters awareness during such times.
One states, for instance, "That was all that mattered in the whole existence." The attention becomes so focused on the event that they
report not seeing or hearing anything or anyone. For other athletes,
the noises and movements of the crowd are folded into the totality of
the experience.

Athletes in flow feel that their actions are effortless and spontaneous. Even though one might be making a superhuman effort, at the
moment it feels entirely natural. Players and participants describe the
phenomenon in these ways: "Things happening automatically," "Reactions are quicker—things just seem to happen," "Relying totally on
the feeling senses of my body." One even says, "Felt I was remote-
controlled in a way."

These sensations come about through merging the mental with the
physical processes, creating a unified feeling and an acute sense of
timing of movements. The unified consciousness brought about by
the merging of action and awareness is perhaps the most telling aspect of the flow experience.

Still other athletes mention the sensations of floating and flowing,
of things feeling easy. A sense of lightness and ease of movement is
often mentioned, as the athletes experience changed perceptions of
effort and of their physical body in space. Because of the very demanding physical nature of some sports, it is often the case that the
athlete feels exhausted, aching, almost unable to move a muscle from
one moment to the next. Marathon runners, long-distance swimmers,
and cross-country skiers, for example, must draw on enormous reserves of will and stamina to complete their events. And yet, even
among these most excruciating ordeals, athletes describe moments
when they are able to ignore the pain and enter an effortless rhythm
that transforms the agony into ecstasy. Often, athletes refer to such
times as "being in the zone."

The experience of merging the self with the actions one is performing provides very positive feelings, often leaving the athlete feeling on
a high. Recalling these moments brings back the positive emotions of

flow and can be a source of motivation, providing a blueprint for returning again to the optimal state.

FLOW COMPONENT #3—CLEAR GOALS

Goals direct action and provide focus. Athletes and coaches use goal setting to help get where they want to go, both for the long and the short term. To enter flow, goals should be clearly set in advance, so that the athlete knows exactly what he is to do. As the activity progresses, an athlete then knows moment-by-moment what to do next—and is more likely to experience flow. This is because clarity of intention helps to focus attention and avoid distraction. Because what is required is clearly spelled out, there is no need to second-guess or doubt what one is doing.

This mind-set is facilitated by knowing exactly what it is you are trying to accomplish. Visualizing the performance ahead of time is one way to keep your mind focused on clear goals. Simon describes the clarity of intent he achieved by visualizing exactly what he was going to do before his race; he relates, "You can almost touch or know that you can predict the outcome of the event before it actually happens."

Hand in hand with a clarity of intent is a moment-by-moment awareness of what is to be done throughout the event. For the final stage of a road race he was leading, Simon mentioned having several goals. They included staying near the front; concentrating for the whole duration of the stage, reacting quickly to any attacks; knowing exactly which riders went in any breakaways; keeping at least seven riders in view at all times (as he had to maintain a certain position to keep his leader's jersey); and, with his teammates, keeping the race under control as much as possible at the start of the final climb. Then it was up to Simon to go all out for the final kilometers, which he did, going on to win the stage and the race. The cyclist, in retelling his goals, mentioned how he was constantly monitoring them throughout the three hours of the race. Moment by moment Simon knew what he had to do and felt he had an endless supply of energy to cope with everything. His attention was focused on his goals, and monitoring them felt, in his words, "like second nature."

When athletes describe optimal sport experiences, two themes related to goals stand out. The first is a clear blueprint of what one is supposed to do, illustrated by these statements: "I knew exactly how I was going to swim the race" and "I knew what I had to do." Second, athletes often report having the intuition before an event that their performance is going to be good. They report "being confident of a quick time," "seeing yourself doing exactly what you plan to do," and "I knew at a certain point that I was going to take off and there would be no stopping me," illustrating their positive convictions.

Knowing in advance what one is going to do occurs at the immediate level as well as in more long-range terms, as illustrated by this football player: "There was one stage when I went up to catch a ball, and I knew when he kicked it, I was going to catch it." Of course, such "knowledge" need not be objectively justified. Often the athlete is wrong, and things don't turn out the way he expected. But in terms of providing a subjective assurance of a favorable outcome, such knowledge helps focus the mind on the activity and helps set the stage for the flow experience. Chapter 5 describes in more detail how to set clear goals that facilitate flow.

FLOW COMPONENT #4— UNAMBIGUOUS FEEDBACK

It would be impossible to participate in any sport if one didn't know, moment by moment, how things were going or how one was doing. A tennis player who couldn't see where his shots were landing or a skier who couldn't tell whether she was on or off the trail would soon give up trying. Feedback describes the knowledge about performance that athletes receive, allowing for continuity in pursuit of their goals.

Feedback is critical to successful performance, and athletes who are tuned into the feedback given by their own movements and bodies, as well as by external cues in the environment, are able to remain connected with what they are doing and in control of where they are headed.

Knowing that "everything was exactly right," having things "go like clockwork" or "go perfectly," provides athletes with cues that they are on track and clearly headed toward their goals. Another expression participants use to describe the feeling of in-tune performance is that "everything clicks." In flow, the individual knows what she wants, and as the performance unfolds she knows that she is on target for achieving her goals. Feedback is continuous, as are the goals that keep the athlete moving forward.

The type of feedback athletes can tune into can come from many different sources. First, and probably most important, is the feedback the body itself provides, particularly in the form of kinesthetic awareness or knowledge of where it is in space. Being aware of the quality of a performance as it occurs and of how it matches an ideal performance is a skill that allows athletes to know moment by moment whether they are creating the movements they want. They can then make adjustments as required to maintain or return to an optimal level.

Feedback can also be external to the performer. One of the advantages of sport is the number of potential sources of feedback it can provide. There are usually other competitors or participants that tell us how we are doing. The coaching staff is able to give advice during performance or during breaks. Spectators provide feedback by heckling or applauding. The setting in which the event takes place and the equipment can also provide feedback. For example, a swimmer knows by the feel of the arms and body through the water whether he is creating a smooth stroke or, alternatively, too much drag. A tennis player knows when she swings the racket whether her positioning is correct or needs adjusting.

Simon explains that when his attention is focused on his goals, monitoring these goals feels like second nature. This automatic response to what is happening around one occurs when the feedback is coming clearly and immediately, as it does in a flow state. During a road race the following things mattered most to Simon—and he was able to obtain quick and clear feedback about how he was doing from taking in the information given by these factors:

> What gear you're riding; what position you're sitting in; where the second, third, fourth, and fifth riders are sitting in the bunch; what numbers are in the breakaway; how many riders there are in front of you—all these things take your attention.

Simon relied on these pieces of information to help him assess how well he was doing in relation to his goals and to stay in tune with his performance, the next flow dimension to be discussed. The importance of feedback and more details about obtaining and using it to facilitate flow are taken up in chapter 6.

FLOW COMPONENT #5— CONCENTRATION ON THE TASK AT HAND

When goals are clear, feedback immediate, and your abilities engaged by an appropriate challenge, you still need all the attention you can muster to attend to what must be done. If you're a skier shooting down a difficult slope, you cannot afford to think about your job or your love life at that moment; if your attention drifts away from the run even for an instant, chances are you will find yourself up to your

neck in snow. The wrestler whose mind wanders will be lying on the mat, and the runner who thinks too far back or too far ahead will lose the rhythm of her pace. Focus in flow is complete and purposeful, with no extraneous thoughts distracting from the task at hand.

Athletes talk about being focused on doing their job, on the movements they are trying to create, of being switched on and maintaining their concentration over a long period of time. Other themes include being aware of where the competitors are, being aware of the big picture, and of hearing people but perceiving them to be of no influence or effect. At first glance, these latter claims may not seem to fit so easily with an idea of total concentration on the task, but they do describe a task focus for some athletes in particular situations. In a middle-distance track race, for example, part of the task is to be aware of where other competitors are, and in team sports such as football or hockey it is most important to be able to keep track of what is happening around you.

Hearing the crowd may not indicate a lack of focus but rather being so totally in tune with the event that even the stadium and its occupants become a part of one's total experience. In flow there is no room for any thoughts other than what you are doing and feeling right at the moment, the "now." If during a cycle race you pour all your energy into the bike—grasping the handlebars, straining at the pedals, tuning the gears—it follows that the reality you experience is that of muscles, lungs, and nerves working together with metal and rubber as one unit. In fact, as far as you know, you have become one with the machine and with the rhythm of the race.

In cycling, road races can last several hours. Nevertheless it is possible to keep the mind concentrated even in difficult conditions, as Simon recalled experiencing in one race:

> I rode for four hours one day in the rain and sleet, and I don't think I remember anything other than the white line on the road, going underneath for four hours. And the guy's wheel in front of me. For four hours, that's all I remember.

Despite this seemingly narrow focus, Simon described being able to take in everything that was happening around him, explaining that he felt he was seeing with a wide-angle lens, taking in a lot more than he usually did but without even being aware of looking around.

Concentration is a critical component and one of the characteristics of optimal experience mentioned most often. Learning to exclude irrelevant thoughts from consciousness and instead to tune into the task at hand is a sign of a disciplined mind. Being able to exclude all the distracting events happening around your performance is not easy, but it is an important skill to master if you want to experience flow in sport. Chapter 7 discusses in more detail how to achieve and maintain concentration in your activity.

FLOW COMPONENT #6— SENSE OF CONTROL

Simon remembers achieving an "unshatterable self-esteem" during the race he just described, feeling that he could take on anything and be able to get through it. This race stood out from other races in many ways, including the sense of having unlimited resources that would allow him to cope with whatever came his way. This sense of control over what you have to do describes the sixth characteristic of flow.

Remembering what it is like to be in the flow state, people report feeling they could do no wrong. Like a feeling of invincibility, the sense of control frees the athlete from fear of failure and creates a feeling of empowerment for the challenging tasks to be executed. More than actually being in control, it is knowing that if you try hard, you *can* be in control: you trust your skills and you know that the task is doable. The outcome of this knowledge is a sense of power, confidence, and calm.

Some athletes refer directly to feeling in control, others to positive thoughts or confidence. The can-do-no-wrong idea comes through in descriptions of feeling "unbeatable," "like I can do anything—[having] no fear," and "like nothing can go wrong." Total composure is indicative of feeling in control. These feelings can occur even when the challenges seem incredibly high to an external observer. For example, a swimmer lining up for an Olympic final said, "I wasn't even fazed by all the other people there, including the world record holder, and the fact that I'd beaten the previous world record holder in the heat." This race turned out to be a very special one for the swimmer who made these comments, with an excellent result made even sweeter by the sense of flow experienced while swimming.

The sense of control comes from a person's belief that he or she has the required skills for the task at hand. It results in a lack of worrying about different possibilities, particularly the possibility of failure, which rarely enters the mind of an athlete in flow. Although the relationship between control and flow is described more fully in chapter 8, we should mention here that it is a delicately balanced connection. Too much control or seeking of control actually pushes one out of flow. Too little control, and again one is less likely to be in flow—and, in such a case, more likely to be experiencing anxiety.

FLOW COMPONENT #7—
LOSS OF SELF-CONSCIOUSNESS

Concern for the self disappears when one is in flow, as do worries or negative thoughts. There is simply no attention left over to worry about the things that in everyday life we usually spend so much time dwelling on. Flow frees the individual from self-concern and self-doubt. Loss of self-consciousness is an empowering characteristic: after the flow experience, the perception of self is stronger and more positive. Relinquishing worries about the self for a period of time is also refreshing and liberating.

Perhaps paradoxically, it is through a sense of control that loss of self-consciousness is facilitated. Simon explains that when you feel in top form, you can let go of worrying about how others see you and whether you have what it takes to be successful. The intimate connection with the performance leaves him no self-doubt, instead providing him moment by moment with a *sureness* about what to do and feedback that everything is on track.

This dimension is closely aligned with the merging of action and awareness—not worrying about oneself frees the self to become totally involved in the activity. Similarly, being one with the activity prevents thoughts related to the self from creeping in and disturbing the moment. When athletes speak of becoming one with the activity, they are also referring to freeing themselves of self-consciousness.

The theme of doing things instinctively is one way in which athletes allude to this dimension. For example, a rugby player spoke of "being very involved, but at an instinctive level"; a triathlete described getting "lost in what I was doing." A particularly insightful way of expressing the loss of self-consciousness was given by a cyclist who called it a "subconscious expression or release—my conscious mind was not interfering." Because of the close connection between three flow dimensions—action-awareness merging, the loss of self-consciousness, and time transformation—these characteristics are discussed together in chapter 4.

FLOW COMPONENT #8—
TRANSFORMATION OF TIME

Being aware of time is a nemesis that today's lifestyle tosses at us. We continually refer to our watches to gauge how much time we have left or how much time there is until some better event starts for us. Time

dependence is a burden that can prevent us from becoming truly involved in what we are doing.

Flow has the potential to free us from this pressure: one of the characteristics of being in flow is having a transformed sense of the way time proceeds. Generally what is experienced in flow is a shortening of time, so that hours pass by like minutes, or minutes like seconds. The reverse can also occur, with minutes seeming to stretch into luxurious longer periods, providing the perception of having all the time in the world for the actions to be performed.

Athletes report both that time seems to slow down and to speed up in flow. Having time to think is one way athletes describe the altered perception. For others, it seems more like a disorientation in time, as they combine ideas of time's slowing and time's speeding. This disorientation seems to be what Simon describes in a track event when 11 seconds went by as if happening in slow motion, but still felt as if they occurred in an instant:

> It felt like you'd slowed everything down and made sure everything was right, everything was fluent. . . . It felt real quick, but everything felt slow at the same time.

The transformation of time that sometimes occurs in flow may seem contradictory: depending on the event and the way the athlete approaches it, time is experienced differently. So for some people it seems as if time slows on some occasions, while at other times the hours pass by like minutes. The experience of an ultra-endurance racer illustrates the sense of time passing quickly:

> For sixteen and a half hours I was in it [flow] basically. If you ask me, did that feel like sixteen and a half hours? I'd say it felt like about three hours.

For events, such as a track sprint, that involve speed and require quick reactions it is probable that time will appear to lengthen in the flow state, providing a seemingly longer opportunity to respond in an appropriate fashion. When events last for many hours, as an ultra-endurance ride does, total absorption may make it seem that things are going much more quickly than they actually are, thus keeping the athlete's effort and concentration in focus for as long as it is necessary.

It seems that the transformation of time is a by-product of total concentration. When you are focused entirely on a task, you cannot keep track of the passing of time, which, when you reflect back on the event, can lead to altered perceptions of how the time has passed. When you are concentrating, you can forget time, so that an event may seem to have finished "before you knew it." The slowing down of time can also be related to concentration: when your mind is really focused, you pick things up with more clarity. For example, a fast-pitched softball coming toward your bat can seem to slow—as you notice even the seams and the curve of the ball—all in a matter of milliseconds before the bat makes contact.

Not all athletes report time transformation. Losing the sense of ordinary time may depend on whether keeping track of time is part of the sport task. A swimmer in a race, for example, may be aware of each second passing because part of her challenge is to keep track of time so she can save her energy for the right moment in the race. So this dimension of flow may not be as universally experienced as others. When the transformation of time is experienced, however, it can feel very liberating to live in a *timeless* moment.

FLOW COMPONENT #9— AUTOTELIC EXPERIENCE

What is an *autotelic* experience? It is one that is intrinsically rewarding, one that we choose to do for its own sake. Flow is an autotelic experience; this was the term first used, in fact, to denote moments of full involvement (see chapter 1). It is a dimension that athletes endorse strongly, and it is what makes flow so enticing that, once experienced, it is sought after again and again.

Athletes use a wide range of terms to describe the fun aspect of flow. Some mention how enjoyable the experience is as it occurs, with statements such as, "It felt great the whole way," "[It was] good fun," and "[It] felt like such a rush." Others focus on how the movements feel great, so that you "feel like a champion—like a true athlete" or you experience the "exhilaration of movements—a buzz." Still other athletes describe this dimension as feeling no pain, feeling strong, having endless supplies of energy, or enjoying the effort.

The perception of performing perfectly is another component of enjoyment and a result of being in flow. Athletes report being left on a high, feeling great, and that they have experienced something tremendously rewarding. "It gives you the buzz to keep doing what you're doing," "What you get out of it far exceeds what you put in," and "Knowing it can happen keeps you going through the bad times" are statements showing clearly that flow is both highly valued and extremely rewarding to those fortunate enough to experience it.

Autotelic experience, discussed more fully in chapter 9, is the end result of the other eight components of flow. Flow is so rewarding that athletes speak of staying on a high for long periods of time afterward. "You can't come down," Simon states simply. Everything seemed positive to the cyclist after winning a long and difficult stage race in which he experienced flow. Even having to drive 10 hours immediately after the race he'd won was a special experience, as he explains:

> We got straight into the car and drove back across Germany and it [the euphoria] lasted all the way. That was the shortest trip of my life. Usually it's a 10-hour drive. I didn't even worry about having to drive 10 hours through the middle of the night and get to bed at 4 o'clock in the morning. It was like no worries! And we couldn't stop [at that hour] at a shop to get anything. It didn't bother me in the slightest. "No, I don't need anything to drink or eat, I'm fine." And you feel like you want to go ride, ride up the hill again.

Such exceptional experiences are there for everyone, not just elite cyclists or other professional athletes. The memory of flow experiences becomes a beacon that shows us the way back from the buffeting waves into a safe haven. Simon describes its powerful effect this way:

> There's nothing, there's no experience in sport that is as exhilarating or rewarding as being in flow. That's what is *it*. That's what makes me keep riding, knowing that I might get it again.

Flow provides a glimpse of perfection, which is why we seek it again and again once we attain it. So, is there a way of finding flow in sport? These nine distinguishing characteristics we have just detailed describe what flow is like. They also hold the keys for how to improve the quality of experience in your favorite physical activity. A detailed analysis of how each of these dimensions contributes to making sport a more worthwhile activity is presented next in part II.

Experiencing
Flow

PART II

3

Finding Your Challenge-Skills Balance

"You always miss 100 percent of the shots you don't take."

If you ask the average person, "What would it take to make you happy?" the typical responses might mention health, money, or a comfortable life in the lap of luxury. Nevertheless, contrary to these deep-seated beliefs, research shows that the most memorable and happy moments in people's lives usually involve a job well done that required skills and concentration or a struggle to overcome a difficult obstacle. People are happy when they have a purpose and are actively involved in trying to reach a challenging goal. When there is nothing to do, no amount of money or expensive possessions makes a person happy.

It seems that evolution has provided us with a powerful survival mechanism: the feeling of joy we experience when we overcome a challenge. It is because of this built-in reward system that explorers are motivated to risk their lives reaching new continents or new planets, that inventors work for years in hopeless poverty to perfect a new machine, or that artists struggle to express a unique vision on a canvas. If we did not derive enjoyment from seeking out and mastering challenges, we would likely spend our time picking lice out of our hair—together with the chimpanzees, with whom we share 98 percent or so of our genes. It is the joy we get from stretching physical and mental potentialities in new directions that motivates human creativity and results in the accomplishments that make us different from any other form of life.

These two dimensions of experience—challenges and skills—refer to basic conditions of consciousness. "Challenge" is really shorthand for a broader concept, which might best be expanded to "opportunities for actions" or "situational demands." Consider, for example, a person locked in a bare room who may lack any external challenges: he might still ponder the challenge of planning to escape from the room, of playing a chess game in his head, or of remembering the words of a song. The concept of "skills" is also rather broad, referring to one's ability to act or the capacity to deal with a situation. It takes specific skills, of course, to play with a kitten, listen to classical music, or make a 90-meter ski jump with elegance. In the most general sense, however, we could use the shorthand term *skills* to refer to all such abilities.

As well as the challenges and skills being well-matched for flow to occur, both factors have to be relatively high for the particular individual. The starting point for flow is likely to occur when challenges and skills go beyond a person's average levels.

THE CHALLENGE-SKILLS QUADRANTS

The "flow" quadrant in figure 3.1 illustrates this CS balance, and it is under this condition that the experience of flow typically occurs. The other quadrants in the figure refer to non-optimal states that come about when there is an imbalance between a person's challenges and skills or when both are at low levels. The top left quadrant is called "anxiety," which describes the feeling one tends to have when challenges are perceived to be higher than one's skills. We can all remember occasions during sport when we have been struck by anxiety. Probably we were in a situation in which we lacked confidence in our ability to be successful, which is another way to describe what happens to our feelings when we perceive that the challenges outweigh our skills.

The bottom two quadrants in figure 3.1 also describe common conditions in sports. "Relaxation-boredom," in the bottom right, is the result of high skills and low challenges. When playing a weaker opponent, a more highly skilled athlete often relaxes and may even

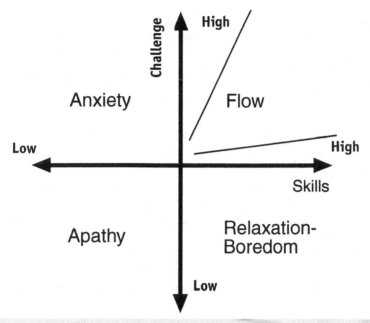

Figure 3.1   Model of the flow state (adapted from Csikszentmihalyi and Csikszentmihalyi, 1988).

experience boredom, due to the lack of perceived challenge in this competitive situation. Athletes are likely to experience "apathy" in situations where neither skills nor challenges are present to a significant level, creating a feeling of low energy levels, boredom, and lack of attention. Monotonous practicing of basic skills can leave one feeling apathetic, and much of the waiting between events, suiting up, or traveling between meets will also produce that feeling.

We now focus on the challenge side of the equation, later looking more closely at the skills side and at assessing and acknowledging the skills we each have.

THE CHALLENGE SIDE OF THE FLOW EQUATION

In most people's lives, meaningful opportunities for action are in short supply. Teenagers feel bored with family and school, and all too often their parents feel the same way about their jobs and home life. This is where sport comes in: for many people, physical activity provides the clearest and most concrete experiences of overcoming challenges.

There are three main ways that sport provides opportunities to overcome challenges. The first and most obvious is the way our bodies balk at exercise—through the very resistance they have to physical exertion. Flow is not the only source of motivation in our lives: more ancient and powerful even than the rewards of overcoming challenge is the pleasure of homeostasis, of seeking out comfort and satiety. There is a "couch potato" in all of us, trying to get us to sit still, be quiet, and conserve energy. All of us must overcome this built-in inertia before we can engage in sport, and often this first obstacle stymies our best intentions.

The second challenge is to become better and better at what we are doing. This involves improving against competitors and, more importantly, against our own previous performances. Sport is so conducive to flow in part because it never fails to provide challenges: There is always room for improving one's performance. With this activity, we're assured of never running out of challenges. When one goal is reached, we can always start looking for a higher level, a fresh opportunity.

Third, sport involves an element of risk. In rock climbing, for example, the risk can be high: losing one's life. In skiing the safety of one's limbs is at stake. In practically every sport *some* element of danger exists—to one's ego, if nothing else. Mastering such risks not only provides flow at the moment but also builds that sense of self-confidence and assurance that is one of the outcomes of overcoming challenges.

> Downhill skier Picabo Street felt motivated by other people's skepticism: "When someone tells me there is only one way to do things, it always lights a fire under my butt. My instant reaction is 'I'm going to prove you wrong.'"

Athletes who are good at finding new opportunities for action in whatever they do, and who are prepared to put themselves on the line, are more able to set the stage for flow to occur than athletes who simply follow routines and play it "safe." Taking risks puts you *on the edge* of the challenge-skills balance equation, extending challenges (and thus skills) beyond comfort zones.

Some people thrive on living beyond the comfort zone, seeming to find satisfaction only from extreme danger. Such people accomplish more than most, but they also tempt dire consequences more than most would care to. Mountain climbers set one more difficult goal after another, with such peaks as Mount Everest being considered the ultimate. An accomplished climber and writer, Jon Krakauer, was a

© Anthony Neste

member of one of the four ill-fated 1996 Everest expeditions that claimed nine lives in the course of a day's climbing. In his account of the Everest tragedy, *Into Thin Air*, Krakauer wrote:

Achieving the summit of a mountain was tangible, immutable, concrete. The incumbent hazards lent the activity a seriousness of purpose that was sorely missed from the rest of my life. I thrilled in the fresh perspective that came from tipping the ordinary plane of existence on end.

Facing the risks of mountaineering is not for everyone, but finding activities where the ever changing CS balance is tipped in favor of challenges provides opportunity for growth—and opportunity for flow.

> Hall of Famer and one of baseball's all-time great base steal-ers Lou Brock understood the importance of living—and playing—on the edge. He made things happen for his St. Louis Cardinals' offense. Rather than waiting for a team-mate to get a hit, Brock advanced around the bases, appar-ently fearless that he might be tagged out. As he said, "Show me a guy to look bait, and I'll show you a guy you can beat every time."

To what extent do *you* seek out new opportunities, new challenges when you participate in sports? Can you think of what challenges you have either created or found as an athlete, coach, or spectator? Chal-lenge is a guiding axis on the flow road map, and by understanding the opportunities in the activities you participate in, you will have a much better understanding of how to create flow in your activities.

Challenge as the Path to Flow

In order to understand how challenge leads to flow, it is useful to refer back to the flow model (see figure 3.1). Flow is predicted to occur when the individual's challenges are above his or her personal average, but also in line with perceived skills (provided these are also above average). So, according to flow theory, people are always seeking to progress fur-ther along the flow channel created by the match between challenges and skills. That is because when they are in the flow channel, individuals experience enjoyment and optimal quality. If they instead stay at their present levels of skills and choose low challenges, they will end up be-coming bored. Whether someone experiences boredom or anxiety will depend on the relative level of challenges versus the individual's skills.

For a time people might continue participating in an activity that is boring most of the time, but it is unlikely they will keep doing it for long. Boredom is one of the reasons why young athletes drop out of their sports. And it is why experienced athletes, seemingly stuck at a certain level, give up their involvement or turn their attention toward another activity.

Learning how to create challenge is important to continued development within any area of involvement. Sport is all about setting and striving for new challenges. Fortunately, it provides many opportunities for doing so.

Creating Challenge in Sport

Sport comes with predefined challenges—in the forms of rules, competitions, equipment, dimensions of the playing surface, and even the behaviors expected to go along with certain events. It is because sport has clearly defined challenges that it is a context where flow can be readily experienced. However, there are many moments when challenges may not be well defined or understood. This ambiguity can make it difficult to experience flow. A coach or teacher can help ensure that an individual is clear on his or her role and knows what the important challenges are in every situation. But in the last analysis, it is important that each athlete learn how to find new challenges when boredom threatens to set in. Beyond what the structure of sport activities provide, there are the many possible challenges or opportunities for action that a sport participant can create for herself or himself.

A few years ago Sue took up the sport of rock climbing. Climbing presented many challenges, but for Sue one especially stood out: managing the anxiety she experienced when she felt insecure or unable to proceed any farther up a climb. Having studied sport anxiety, she knew the symptoms all too well: sweaty palms and feet, increased heart rate, dry mouth, physical trembling in the legs and feet. Previously she had taken part in sports that contain fewer obvious risks, so she had never before experienced quite the levels of anxiety she felt on the rock face. Sport climbing is actually a safe activity when done correctly. But knowing this did little to calm her nervous limbs and racing mind, confronted with challenges she perceived as dangerous. She was depending on skills that she was uncertain of. Once Sue had reasoned with herself that her fear was irrational (after taking a fall and surviving!) and focused instead on the next hold she had to reach, she began to find herself moving effortlessly from one move to the next.

The key was to define an appropriate challenge and focus only on it. The challenges Sue defined were far different from the ones her climbing companions (experienced instructors of the sport) had at the time. She might focus on getting up a pitch on top rope—while their challenge would be to lead the climb. Top-roping and leading are different worlds in climbing, and certainly leading objectively presents a much greater challenge in the form of physical and mental risk. On top rope, the climber is attached to a belayer who will quickly stop any fall; when leading, a climber relies on occasional protection in the rock to arrest her fall.

Rock climbing provides clearly differentiated levels of challenge in the grading of climbs and the choice of top-roping or lead climbing. To these challenges can also be added the weather and different environmental conditions. Mountaineering combines the challenges of climbing with ascending and descending very difficult terrain, often in unfavorable weather, thus adding levels of complexity to the task.

In some sports with structured challenges, the grading or characteristics of the activity itself change once the athletes' performances surpass the highest set standards. For example, in artistic gymnastics, which relies on a code of points for measuring the challenge and skill level of gymnasts, the degree of difficulty of certain moves is regraded downward after a period of time, and gymnasts are required to perform increasingly more complex moves in order to score well. The code of points by which the sport is judged is revised upward periodically, lifting the sport to ever increasing levels of difficulty.

In sports in which the structured challenges remain fairly constant, however, athletes themselves can change the challenges they perceive by finding unique opportunities for demonstration of skill. Dennis Rodman of the Chicago Bulls made the skill of rebounding an art; he sets his own challenges for his play within the greater challenges of the game. "I rebound with a little flair, a little something extra," says Rodman. "It's not for the crowd; it's just for me. Rebounding is how I express myself on the floor." By thinking creatively and focusing on areas of strength, athletes and coaches can keep pushing the challenge axis of the flow channel upward.

KEYS TO FLOW CHALLENGE

You face hurdles even before you choose your challenges. Most hurdles can be seen in a positive or negative light, however, like the proverbial two sides of the coin. Let's look at a few of the common hurdles and how athletes tackle them. These are the keys to challenge. To enjoy sport at its best, we have to learn to find as many opportunities to act and perfect performance as possible—sometimes finding them in the most unlikely places. Using these keys will help an athlete view challenges positively.

Get Moving—Overcome Inertia

It is much easier not to exert yourself than to get actively involved in sport, so the first challenge is simply getting off the couch. This is less of a problem for athletes who participate in organized sport and have regularly scheduled events and training sessions. But for people who have all the good intentions to practice sport on their own, just getting started is often the main hurdle to overcome. In studies of teenagers, for instance, we find that they are much happier when they do sport than when they are involved in passive leisure activities, such as watching TV or hanging out at the mall. Sport and active leisure provide flow-like experiences almost half of the time, whereas watching TV approximates flow less than one time out of six. So one would expect that young people would do sport more often than watch TV, right? Of course the opposite is what happens: American teens on the average spend at least four times more time watching TV than in being physically active.

So why are they investing so little time in sport, which makes them feel so much happier? The explanation they give is simple: turning on a TV set is a lot easier than getting ready for a game of basketball or changing into cycling gear or taking a bus to the swimming pool.

All sports require an initial investment of energy on our part before we start reaping the benefit of flow from performance. In a sense, one must pay some dues—time, effort, preparation—whereas passive entertainment comes free. Many people are unable to make that investment of energy up front, and so they never get to experience the joy of sport. Passive leisure, while it demands little from us, provides little joy and little in the way of enhancing the self.

Clearly, one of the major impediments to experiencing flow in sport is getting past the often boring preparation required to initiate an activity. This takes harnessing your energy. It is important to realize that you are not going to keep up the involvement necessary to practice a sport unless you develop a habitual schedule. If you don't belong to a club or have your own personal trainer or coach, you have to build a schedule on your own.

Like it or not, we are creatures of habit. The only sure way to keep up with a regimen that requires effort is to make it such a predictable part of your week or your day that to miss it would take even more effort than would just doing what you have to do. At first, you might have to force yourself to run four miles before breakfast each morning; after a while, if these four miles become a habit, breakfast will not taste right if you've missed your run. It is useful to build a ritual around your scheduled periods of exercise. If you put your own stamp on these routines—if you personalize your clothes, your equipment, the stretching exercises, the shower afterward—they become easy, and you can slip effortlessly into the flow of sport.

Face Down Failure

Seeking challenge is not only essential for flow; it is also part of being human. We face challenge at every move to the next level of complexity, be it the infant learning to walk or the pole-vaulter learning to place his pole correctly to generate the best flight trajectory. Yet as we face challenges of increasing complexity, we are also socialized to make choices that will optimize our chances of success. We learn that failure is to be avoided—for often with failure comes negative evaluation.

Some individuals learn to equate failure *at a skill or activity* with their own failure as competent people. This is particularly evident in sport, where athletes are continually being evaluated on performance outcomes. When this becomes the main, or even only, source of feedback an athlete receives, he can come to view himself as "athlete" rather than as a person who takes part in athletics. The consequences of failing in athletics then take on greater proportions, being intimately tied up with a sense of self-worth as a person.

By changing our primary focus from achieving certain outcomes to creating opportunities for optimal experiences, however, the consequences of failure are dulled at the same time as the potential for success is enhanced.

Relishing the Challenge

Jack Nicklaus, one of golf's greats, had this to say about the challenge of close competition:

> "The tougher and closer the competition, the more I enjoy golf. Winning by easy margins may offer other kinds of satisfaction, but it's not nearly as enjoyable as battling it out shot by shot right down to the wire."

Move Beyond the Comfort Zone

A fear of failure holds some people back from embracing challenge and improving their skills. Challenge involves the risk of not succeeding. Complacency may be a *symptom* of the fear of failure; for some individuals, complacency occurs because of their preference for staying within the comfort zone of performance. While comfort and ease may be appropriate when sport is used as a form of relaxation, they do not make a good mind-set for athletes trying to achieve new skill levels or improve. It is not possible to go forward while seeking to maintain a comfortable feeling about performance.

Complacency can also come about from being overly confident of one's ability to meet the challenge. When superior athletes are matched against weaker opponents, it is not uncommon for the more highly skilled players to find themselves struggling in situations where the objective challenges seem lower than their skills. Whereas the weaker players find the challenge of superior opponents lifts their performance, the apparent ease of outperforming a lesser-skilled opponent can actually become a challenge of sorts for the complacent star who has let his focus slip. Tennis matches provide clear illustrations of the effects of complacency on highly ranked professional players. Few top tennis players are immune to first-round losses to lower-ranked opponents. To prevent the upset from occurring, when star athletes play against someone of lesser rank, they need to define new challenges other than simply gaining a victory (such as focusing on specific ways to improve their own game).

Some athletes continually strive to improve their skills and performances, always seeking to push the boundaries of accomplishment. Placing performance in the context of competition encourages this extension of skills, but even without this incentive of matching skills against others, athletes who enjoy their sport usually can be found to be setting increasingly higher challenges for themselves. Flow theory can help you understand this positive attitude toward challenge, because with increasing challenge comes the opportunity for optimal experiences.

How do athletes extend their limits? There are many ways they go about this, which can be divided into two main categories: person-centered and environment-centered. An athlete can change the challenge of a situation by changing her thoughts or how she perceives the situation. A tennis player matched against a weaker opponent may not find much challenge in trying to win the match. By changing the focus from winning to her own game and setting goals for different components of her game, the tennis player can continue to be challenged throughout the match. It is important to keep in mind that it is the *perception* of challenges that is important for flow, not what the apparent objective challenge of a situation may appear to be.

Just as it is possible to increase the challenges by adjusting personal goals, so too can an athlete lower the challenges when faced with a situation too far above her present skill level. For the weaker tennis player in the match, winning may not be an appropriate goal. It may even hinder this player from experiencing flow if the challenge is too far above her current skill level. This player can set her own personal goals, nevertheless, so that the challenge will not be overwhelming. Returning a superior opponent's first serve into play may provide a suitable challenge for this player, and even though winning is not likely, flow can still be experienced if her challenges and skills are evenly matched.

Changing the environment is another way to alter the challenges an athlete faces. As with skills, the environment can be modified to increase or decrease challenges. Aspects of an athlete's environment that can be modified include the size or dimensions of the playing or performing area, the amount of input an athlete is expected to cope with, the extent of external distractions or interference, or the presence or attitude of an audience. There are many ways to modify the environment so that challenges are set at a level just above an individual's current skill level. Successful coaches do this all the time in practices. Learning physical skills often follows a part-whole approach, where the final skill to be learned is broken down into smaller components, each one of which is practiced independently; gradually these are incorporated with other components, until the whole skill can be successfully performed.

Sport environments can be made more challenging, too, by requiring the skills to be performed under some handicap. A basketball player may be allowed to shoot only from behind the three-point line; a runner may choose a very hilly course to train on. Constant attention to the person-centered challenges and the challenges of the environment help ensure that an appropriate level of challenge is present so that an athlete is encouraged to extend himself toward higher performance.

Unplanned Challenges

Sometimes the environment presents challenges that are not planned but that require some adaptation for success to occur. One champion figure skater told a funny story that he associated with flow. By turning a very distracting and potentially dangerous situation into a challenge, the skater used his determination to keep his focus on what he had to do when, skating in the Olympics, he faced a unique challenge:

> All of a sudden the plan changed. . . . We've always been the only people out on the ice, but this time a camera man dropped over his camera case and walked out onto the ice to retrieve it at the beginning of our performance! And all of a sudden we weren't alone on the ice. But it was a challenge, and I was in my frame of focus, so I just quickly turned it into a positive. I was getting ready to do the most difficult lift I'd ever made up with my partner, and I had to make a few adjustments 'cause I saw this guy out there. I quickly rechanneled my focus back again to my partner, which I had to do instantaneously because I had this most difficult lift to do. And I just used

it, as in "OK, everyone is going to expect something to go wrong with us. . . . Well, watch this!" I went back to "watch this!" again, which is really strong for me.

Extending limits applies to all levels of sport performers, novices through elite athletes. We often think of highly skilled performers extending their limits by putting themselves on the line and attempting to push past existing records or standards. To be successful at the highest levels of sport it *is* necessary to be able to reach for and endure beyond—by welcoming challenges of one's physical and mental limits. However, a novice performer is also extending her limits when she attempts to go beyond her previous, more elementary level. The absolute, or objective, level may be much different, compared with the world-class athlete's, but the same principle of increasing the challenge applies. How the challenge is perceived is the critical issue.

To perceive challenge in a positive or facilitative way, your self-talk should be positive and energetic. Positive statements like "I can reach that little bit higher" or "I *can* do this!" keep your efforts directed toward accomplishment of the task. It is important that any negative self-talk be stopped and turned around to reflect a positive orientation. To increase effort, you can use words and phrases focusing on energy and power, saying them in a strong and positive way. If concentration is the critical issue, statements that are task-focused can help keep your attention directed. The next chapter discusses the skill of self-talk in more detail.

Extending limits is a key to creating the right level of challenge. A person who is highly motivated to engage in an activity will find it easier to extend his limits than will someone who lacks motivation. The concept of motivation is central to the flow experience (and we address it particularly in chapters 5 and 9, which deal with goals and enjoyment respectively). Challenge is also closely tied to skills. It is when several dimensions of flow come together that optimal experience occurs. Challenge is an important component of flow, but it is the *interconnection of challenge with skills*, along with the positive expression of other flow elements, that creates this optimal experience.

So far we have focused on the vertical axis of the flow model: perceived challenges of an activity, which are central to flow and to productive and enjoyable sport experiences. Challenge can be found in many different aspects of sport, and we have now discussed examples of different types of challenges an athlete may face. Other areas of opportunity that you may want to pursue include perfecting your

equipment, learning about the history of your sport, and getting to know other athletes—their personalities, strengths, and weaknesses.

Table 3.1 presents a typology of sport challenges to show some of the areas in which you can find or create opportunities. You might

Table 3.1

Example Typology of Challenges in Sport

Dimensions of sport challenge	Opportunities for action (challenge)	Examples
Physical	Effort expenditure.	Pacing self in endurance race.
	Development of physical capacities (strength, speed, flexibility, endurance).	Strength training to increase power.
	Development of physical skills (agility, ball skills, anticipation, etc.).	Drills to improve anticipation.
Mental	Development of mental skills (concentration, Imagery, self-talk, etc.).	Imagery routine of aspect of performance.
	Strategy planning.	Game plans.
	Setting clear goals & directing motivation toward goal accomplishment.	Weekly goal-setting exercise & evaluation.
	Persistence.	Feedback & continual practice of difficult skills.
	Knowledge of sport culture & history.	Pregame ritual or routine.
Technique & equipment	Understanding technical requirements of activity.	Reading technical manuals.
	Optimizing equipment.	Consultations with bio-mechanical specialist.
	Personalizing technique or equipment.	Creating your own signature play.
Nutritional & energy requirements	Knowledge of energy demands of activity.	Measurement of energy intake & output.
	Fluid & fuel replacement.	Nutritional analysis.

wish to use this table to analyze your sport in terms of its relevant challenges. You can probably add some other challenges you have discovered to this list. Use this table to build upon the potentialities your sport provides.

THE SKILLS SIDE OF THE EQUATION

Most people believe that material comforts and relaxing leisure are what makes life happy and enjoyable. Heaven on earth, they think, consists in having nothing to do and plenty of entertainment to amuse oneself with. But in the long term this belief is mistaken. Contrary to popular opinion, the most enjoyable and satisfying moments, the ones that make life meaningful and happy, are usually those when we make something happen, when we achieve something difficult by the use of brains or muscle. Although many of us strive to be super-consumers—owning luxurious cars, huge TV sets, going on exotic holidays—the fact is that these are not the things that will make us happy. Consuming entertainment kills time and relieves boredom, but rarely does it make us feel good about ourselves. Life is most exhilarating when we are deeply involved in a complex challenge. The best strategy for enjoying life is to develop whatever skills one has and to use them as fully as possible.

The most fundamental of these skills are physical ones. Each of us first experiences selfhood through controlling the body and its movements; in fact, a baby learns the limits of what he or she can do by reaching, pulling, pushing, crawling, and climbing. The pleasures of running, jumping, diving, and bouncing are among the most basic sources of our sensing human well-being. As we grow up, much of our sense of self develops out of what we know our body can do. We are self-confident if it performs well, shy if it is awkward—and if our body is clumsy, we tend to develop a sense of inferiority.

Believing in Your Skills

It is important to realize that the relationship between physical skills and mental states is not just one-way. Our thoughts influence physical performance just as much as our performance affects the way we think about ourselves. There are thousands of individuals who through accidents have lost the use of their limbs or who were born with congenital defects, but who nevertheless believe in their abilities and, against all odds, develop athletic skills to remarkable levels. This same relationship obtains, in a less dramatic fashion, for each one of us. What skills we have and how well we use them are not just a matter of physical endowment, but also depend on positive attitude and resolution.

It is easy to misunderstand the role of skills in flow. Because the experience is so spontaneous and effortless, many people think that flow does not require the use of skills. They don't realize that, paradoxically, it is only when the skills are so well practiced as to have become automatic that one can abandon oneself to spontaneous action and experience flow. The novice skier on a difficult slope is intensely self-conscious and worried: He is concerned about positioning the edges of the skis so that he can turn without falling. And he is unable to forget himself and glide effortlessly. Only after he has become an expert can he do the turns spontaneously and enjoy the run.

There is an old Italian adage, *Impara l'arte, e mettila da parte,* which translated literally means "Learn the art, and then put it aside." It is good advice not only for artists and craftsmen, but also for experiencing flow in sport: Practice the skills to the point that you can forget you have them. Then abandon yourself to the performance.

Our beliefs about what we can do are a powerful influence on what we attempt in life. Sport involves the development of a range of physical and mental skills, from maximizing bursts of speed to restraining oneself when the strategy indicates that one should conserve energy. How we perceive our potential to develop these skills in the specific sport settings in which we participate has a profound influence on what we ultimately accomplish and how we feel about it. We will give you a technique later in this chapter for developing or improving your self-talk and beliefs about yourself.

Finding the Right Mix of Challenges and Skills

To experience flow in sport requires a progressive development of the skill side of the challenge-skill equation. You will recall that the horizontal axis of the flow model is defined by skill. For flow to occur, skills need to keep pace with the opportunities for action the sport provides. We risk boredom if our skills outweigh the challenges—and anxiety if the challenges are greater than our skills.

Boredom comes about from situations in which we don't find much challenge. Playing a weaker opponent can become boring if the only goal of the stronger athlete is to win. Staying within the comfort zone of performance may be relaxing at first, but eventually it can lead to boredom.

Anxiety is easy enough to recognize. But it can be difficult to lose when athletes are "stuck" in a situation beyond their present skill levels or when they feel either unable or unwilling to decrease the challenge. The all-important CS balance is found only when the right mix of challenges and skills is present.

It's What You Believe It Is

There is a very important point to keep in mind regarding the challenge-skill equation: it is not the objective level of skill or challenge that determines the quality of experience, but our perceptions of these factors. If we believe our skills to be high when some high challenge is present, we are much more likely to have a positive experience and successful outcome than if we doubt our abilities in this situation.

> Perhaps the greatest heavyweight boxer in history, Muhammad Ali, said it best: "It's lack of faith that makes people afraid of meeting challenges, and I believe in myself." Underneath all of Ali's bravado lay that core belief that sustained him through his toughest matches and, later, in the face of health problems.

Of course, if our perceptions are not grounded in an objective skill base, we run the risk of suffering the negative effects of *false confidence*. This might lead an athlete to set a goal that is not realistic. It is much more common, however, to worry that we don't have what it takes when in fact previous performances indicate otherwise.

KEYS TO HAVING CONFIDENCE IN YOUR SKILLS

When confidence is shaky it can become a barrier to experiencing flow. We will explore why confidence is often an unstable factor in sport.

Switch Channels on Unstable Reception

By definition, sport rarely guarantees a successful outcome. The competitive format of sport ensures that for every winner there will be many losers. And there are so many factors outside one's control that can affect the outcome of an event: the weather, your opponents' skills or motivation, the playing surface, your diet, and your mental readiness—just to name a few. The culture of sport places such a great importance on who wins and who loses that it is easy to fall into the error of thinking that these are the only outcomes that matter. Athletes and coaches internalize this orientation through repeated reinforcement of the importance of winning.

The danger comes when the only feedback an athlete or coach uses to assess outcomes is victory or defeat. Winning does not automatically

© Human Kinetics

equate with high-level skills, any more than coming in 2nd, 5th, or 25th necessarily means that one has low skills. If you judge yourself and others in terms of placement alone, unless you always win you are likely to undermine your self-confidence. This, in turn, makes it difficult to experience flow because of the resultant unstable perception of your skills. The feedback you want to pay most attention to is how your performance is progressing in relation to *your personal goals*.

Switch Channels on Nagging Self-Doubts

How many times have you found yourself questioning your abilities in situations where skills are on the line? Although what you are being asked to do may be something you have performed successfully on frequent past occasions, self-doubts can still creep in and unbalance the challenge-skill equation. "Did I prepare enough?" "Do I really have what it takes?" "Maybe last time I was lucky." These are typical ways of doubting your abilities. And making these kinds of self-comments is common when the pressure you perceive is high. When it is down to that last 30 seconds in the game and you are in a position to score a goal, or during the Olympic final when you are trying to summon all your reserves, self-doubts can come alive and throw you into mental turmoil.

Negative thinking can be a hard habit to beat. If it becomes an automatic mode of responding, it can dominate your thinking.

Sue recounts a story where she was faced with negative thoughts in a situation that really demanded belief in herself. Wanting a new challenge in her life, she decided to learn more about flying. She found out about a few of the local flying schools, went out, and obtained some information on what was involved in learning to fly. In choosing flying as a new challenge, Sue knew she was partly influenced by a developing fear of flying. As a passenger on many trans-Pacific flights, she flew—or more correctly, was flown—frequently. But she found herself becoming more and more fearful when turbulence hit, and she decided a good way to overcome this fear would be to learn more about flying and to be at the *controls* of an airplane.

Sue signed up for a trial instructional flight, which would include a preflight briefing, half an hour of flying, and a debriefing. Once at the flying school, she was led straight out to a Cessna 152 and given a headset. The preflight briefing consisted of a walk around the airplane and a quick explanation of the mechanisms and techniques for ascending, descending, and turning—no safety demonstration or talk of safety or what to do in emergencies. Suddenly Sue found herself thinking about how no one knew she was out here. She had decided to take the flight on the spur of the moment. She thought to herself, "What if something goes wrong and I die? No one will even know what has happened or where I am." Instead of listening to the instructor's explanations of how a rudder works, she found herself wondering about crashing before she was even off the ground. Not wanting to back out at the last minute, Sue knew she would have to change this way of thinking.

So, instead of thinking about all the possible things that could go wrong, like a midair collision with another small plane, losing control in turbulence, or the plane simply exploding (all thoughts that had passed through her mind in a matter of moments), Sue switched her focus to trying to understand the task ahead. If she had continued with her negative thoughts, she would have not been able to take the controls and enjoy the experience of flying a plane.

Once in the air Sue was confronted with a new challenge to her confidence. She found she could not clearly make out what her instructor was telling her. After increasing the volume in the headphones and still hearing garbled messages, the instructor explained that the headphones were old and might not be working properly. He had mentioned before they took off that he would instruct her on what to do via the headphones and they would use the statements, "Taking over" and "Handing over" when there was to be an exchange of controls. Her anxiety rose significantly when she heard what sounded like "Handing over" and then a string of commands she could not clearly decipher. She flew more by instinct than instruction and had to keep telling herself that she could do it. In other words, Sue had to overcome her earlier self-talk without help from the information being relayed by the instructor. This example demonstrated to her how powerful what we say to ourselves and others can be in determining confidence, performance, and quality of experience.

Negative statements, whether coming from an outside source or from within, can undo any potential for optimal experience. Coaches have an enormous influence on athletes' mind-sets by what they choose to say before, during, or after an event. But it is not only coaches who influence athletes. Parents, spouses, teammates, spectators, the media, opponents . . . there are so many potential sources for confidence-sapping feedback confronting an athlete that it is no surprise that confidence can be shaky. However, above and beyond all these outside sources of information, the things we say to ourselves have far more power to influence our experience than the combination of all potential outside sources.

The inner voice knows what keys to turn in order to shake us up. This inner critic knows every weakness, and catalogues all our past mistakes so it can throw them back at us when we're confronting a challenge. *Learning to control our self-talk* is a key mental skill for developing confidence.

Have you ever wished you could turn off that voice in your head that tells you all the things you are doing and have done wrong? Through thought-stopping you *can* learn to switch it on and off or to change the channel when the incoming information is not what you want to hear.

Thought stopping is a technique that follows three simple steps. First, pay attention to what you are saying to yourself. Second, when you hear yourself saying or thinking something negative, stop the thoughts by firmly saying to yourself, "Stop!" This in itself often breaks the thought pattern. The third step is to replace the negative stream of thought with a positive line. It is like switching channels on your TV or radio when the incoming station is not what you want to see or hear.

Although thought stopping is a simple and straightforward procedure, like all mental skills it requires regular practice and use in order to be effective. Trying it once and finding yourself slipping back into negative thinking does not mean the technique is ineffective, but rather that you have not yet learned to use it at a level where it will work effectively. The ultimate goal with the skill of thought stopping is to have it work automatically, every time you need it. This is the true test of mental skills: When you're under pressure, do your thoughts turn against you? Or do they come to your aid?

Learning to speak to yourself in a positive way is another useful skill for improving confidence. Talking to yourself is not a sign of impending madness but of self-awareness. Some people are not even aware that they are talking to themselves, while others are all too familiar with their inner voice. A simple exercise follows that will help identify how often and what type of self-talk you use.

Self-Talk Exercise

This exercise will require you to carry a logbook around for the day. Choose a day when you will be practicing your sport or activity. Pay attention to what you say to yourself throughout the day. Whenever you think or say something to or about yourself, jot it down in the logbook. At the end of the day count up the statements you recorded. Next to each one, list whether it is a positive or negative statement by putting a "P" or "N" next to it. Count how many positives and negatives you have. You will now have an idea of how frequently you use self-talk and whether it is working for or against you. If you found you had lots of negative statements, see if you can come up with a positive replacement for each negative and rehearse these positive statements. When you find yourself in a situation similar to one in which your self-talk had been negative, try saying the positive alternative instead. The process is like changing a bad technical habit in a sport. You need to identify the problem behavior, learn a more appropriate behavior, and practice this positive skill often to retrain the body to respond as you want it to.

© Ron Vesely

Preparation and Simulation Training

We have already discussed how preparation is important to experiencing flow. The knowledge that the work has been done and you are ready builds confidence and initiates a positive spiral: preparation leads to confidence, which leads to flow. When it is time to compete, knowing exactly what lies before you and not fearing it—instead actually looking forward to the event—results from confidence in your preparation. Good training lifts the level of confidence when it is time to compete. Here's how a rower describes a race when everything came together for his crew:

> We were just confident that we could do it. Because we'd done it so often in training . . . there was not even a hint of panic or anything like that. . . . It was just a calm, collected approach, even going for the line. It's like we'd done it so many times in simulated training, so we were just doing it here in this situation with other crews around. So it was like clockwork in a way.

Simulation training is a useful tool for many sports. It involves replicating the competition environment in a training situation. The more the actual event can be simulated, including such aspects as crowd noise, uniforms, arousal levels, and so on, the more useful the experience. When the time comes to put your skills to the test, knowing you've done it all before and have been successful is a confidence booster.

The rower in the previous example referred to everything going like clockwork. He is describing another benefit of good preparation—getting to the point where performance occurs at almost an automatic level. When confidence levels are high, you can perform without having to consciously think about every little detail. This frees the mind to become more absorbed with the total performance.

And when that happens, good fortune often comes along with it. As former University of Texas coach Darrel Royal once noted, "Luck is what happens when preparation meets opportunity." In a similar vein, Thomas Jefferson observed almost two hundred years before Royal, "I'm a great believer in luck, and I find the harder I work, the more I have of it."

BALANCING ON THE SLIPPERY CHALLENGE-SKILLS BEAM

One of the most positive aspects of the flow experience is its fluidity. It is not a static but a flexible state. By modifying the level of challenge and skills, almost any situation can be turned into one with potential for flow to occur. Just as you can modify the challenge axis of the equation, you can also change the skills axis, although this usually takes more time. Improving skill levels in your sport, however, will increase the potential for flow experiences.

For elite athletes, the skills factor—or, more correctly, the confidence factor—is often the more critical of the two axes. Challenges are typically high for elite, competitive athletes. Confidence, by comparison, may fluctuate between situations of objectively equal challenge. When asked about what is *most* important for flow, one of the factors elite athletes cite most frequently is confidence. As one competitor put it, "Confidence encompasses everything."

High-level sport involves great stress, particularly when strong expectations are riding on the outcomes of the competition. Confidence can be difficult to attain or retain in the face of pressure, but the ability to do so can lift the experience to flow levels. For when faced with great challenges, athletes have meta-skills working for the production of an optimal experience. Motivation is likely to be high, the habit of concentration will be well developed, and, of course, the technical skills will be in place. When athletes are able to plug high confidence into a high-pressure situation, there is good potential for them to experience flow.

An international rugby player remembers a World Cup final event where flow occurred when his team was able to maintain confidence in the face of extreme pressure:

> Towards the end of the game when there was a lot of pressure from people actually watching the game and thinking we were going to lose . . . I was in a totally relaxed, totally confident state. I wasn't worried at all, and in my mind was saying, "Where are they going to go next? Do we need a defensive position?" There was no panic whatsoever. There was a lot to play for. If we'd lost that, we would have had the wall fall in on us, the whole world would have fallen around our shoulders really. . . . There was enormous pressure, no doubt. But the pressure didn't seem to be in the game. Confidence overcame the pressure.

Apparently, despite the intense pressure to win the game, he and his team were able to turn the stress into a positive factor by matching it with equally high confidence levels. The team went on to win the World Cup final.

By working on improving confidence levels, using ideas like the ones described in this chapter, your skill axis will be able to keep pace with the growing challenges you face as you progress in your sport.

Success Situations

The old adage that nothing breeds success like success is an important principle so far as confidence is concerned. Success may mean the final outcome of an event, but just as likely it can also include your demonstrating a particular new skill or consistency in performance. The number of ways in which sport success can be defined is only limited by how many goals can be set in a particular situation. Each goal provides a yardstick for measuring subsequent success.

Attention to goals thus provides one way of optimizing success experiences. Setting multiple task goals gives a coach and athlete many opportunities to succeed. The coach can structure environments to promote different goals, and the athlete can take control of his own inner environment, that is, the content and intent of his self-talk, to increase his chances for success.

Believing in Yourself

The importance of confidence to flow experiences cannot be stressed enough. While it is possible to modify challenges, sport, through its clear structure and rules, defines to a large extent what the challenges are. Of course, through a personal redefining of challenges, an athlete can find different paths to achieving flow. However, without a belief that "I can withstand challenges that will come from many fronts," flow will remain an elusive experience. Self-belief refers to the core ideas an athlete holds about himself as an athlete. It is built up or eroded away over a period of time as a consequence of the experiences one has in sport and how these are interpreted. Learning to nurture confidence and not let it be at the mercy of the sport environment will ensure that a positive and strong self-belief develops. This will provide a solid foundation from which to build many positive sport experiences.

We finish this chapter with a skills inventory exercise. Think of the important skills applicable to your sport. Remember to include physical, mental, technical, and strategic factors. List these in the first column of table 3.2. In the second column rate the importance of each skill to your success, using a scale of 0 to 10. In the third column, rate your current perception of ability in relation to each skill. Compare your scores across each skill for columns 2 and 3. Hopefully, they will be similar. Where there is a big discrepancy between the scores in columns 2 and 3, with the latter being lower, these are areas for you to focus on building up. Flow occurs when skills and challenges are closely matched and at a *personally* high level, so analyze your ratings according to this idea of CS balance. You can think of column 2 as being challenge scores. Your challenge is to master this skill to the level indicated by your rating. Column 3 represents your perceived skill score. Where are your skill ratings in comparison with your challenge ratings?

Table 3.2		
Personal Skills Inventory		
Skill	*Importance rating (0-10)*	*Perceived skill rating (0-10)*
Physical skills:		
Mental skills:		
Technical skills:		
Strategic skills:		
Other skills:		

4

Transcending Normal Awareness

L iving in the 20th century means having to keep pace with a way of life that is rushed and stressful. The atmosphere is competitive, and employers reward those who push the limits to get ahead. Every minute of the day is filled with things to do, as well as things that should have been done before, and the more things we plan to do, the more potential conflict there is among desirable alternatives. In sports, as well, such dilemmas are quite frequent. "Should I taper for this upcoming race, where I stand a chance to do well, or keep up the heavy training in preparation for my major meet in three months time?" "Am I spending too much time training and neglecting my career or family?"

NORMAL AWARENESS

The constant demands on energy and attention are not conducive to a good quality of life. It's not just that we fail to stop and smell the roses. Often we even fail to notice they are there.

To achieve success in our competitive world requires pushing beyond our limits. And to be successful in high-level sport today requires a commitment that goes beyond normal. The "fast track" is demanding indeed, with athletes and coaches constantly pushing the envelope. Our minds and bodies operate on overdrive. Our thinking flits from one thing to another, chasing new angles and opportunities. We rarely focus on the present because we are too eager to reach what is still to come.

Perhaps even more distracting is that having internalized high standards for success, we continually tell ourselves what we are doing wrong and criticize our performance. If we demand too much of ourselves, doubts and disillusion are certain to follow. Normal awareness can be troubling enough in its frenzied demands, and the serious athlete must learn to deal with extra doubts and self-criticism. That is why in contrast to everyday awareness the experience of flow is so refreshing, its full clarity unclouded by self-consciousness or self-evaluation.

FLOW'S TRANSCENDENT AWARENESS

Flow provides moments of uncluttered thinking and freedom from self-doubts and worries. Total absorption in the task at hand is one of the surest signs of being in flow, and this complete focus stands in contrast to ordinary awareness, where holding a single thought for more than a few moments is difficult. The athlete in flow has a sure sense of what is to be done, and can perform with uninterrupted attention.

> Great professional athletes, such as Wayne Gretzky, Tiger Woods, and Michael Jordan, who are in heavy demand away from their sport say that the course or playing field is the one place they are able to free themselves from distraction and find that special focus. Many refer to it as "escape" from reality, but what they really are saying is that it's their one place of refuge from day-to-day concerns and demands. In fact, it is the one place where their full senses can be honed, where they can be absorbed fully in their activity.

Simon, the cyclist you've read about in earlier chapters, explained how it amazed him that he could maintain such high concentration for periods of three hours or more when he experienced flow during road races. This is how he described his awareness during these times:

> Your awareness of things is running like 180 percent, and it's taking in every little detail, because you know that later on you're going to want

© The Picture Desk

to look back and analyze it. And so even though I was stuck in the job and doing it full on, everything was being recorded.

While describing his total absorption in riding, Simon was at the same time more than usually aware of what was going on around him:

I know I was not looking at the scenery, but the scenery was going with it. Things that you don't usually take a lot of note of, or you haven't got enough mental openness to take in . . . everything is just like a wide-angle lens, and you get more in, and it records better. . . . You notice more, because the personal problems like pain, or lack of recovery, or lack of breath, or anything else take a back seat. And there's a lot more your senses are aware of—[you have] energy to notice other things.

The analogy of a wide-angle lens allowing more information to register illustrates well the increased awareness accompanying flow. Simon also spoke of having more energy to notice things that might normally go unnoticed. Because he was not distracted there was more attention to go around, and instead of being used up in questioning and worrying, it could take in details that ordinarily would go unnoticed.

Being Absorbed in What You Are Doing

What is it like when you are totally absorbed in what you are doing? Do you have a wide-angle lens, allowing you to take in everything around you, or is your focus narrow, including only your immediate area of performance? Describe what happens to your awareness when you become totally absorbed in your performance. Can you think of what helped you get there—or what took you out of this totally absorbed state?

KEYS TO TOTAL ABSORPTION

The transcendence of normal awareness that occurs in flow is a very special experience. However, getting there requires overcoming some high hurdles. Basically you must focus on productively channeling your awareness to your body, the process you're involved in, and to movement itself.

Forget Yourself

Part of being totally absorbed is not having any mental space for worrying about one's self. Letting go of concern for what others are thinking of you is freedom from self-consciousness. Probably the greatest obstacle to being able to experience the absorption of flow, in fact, is your *self*. The loss of self-consciousness that occurs in flow is a liberating experience that is quite distinct from how we normally function. Usually we are all too aware of ourselves—the social persona that we present to others—and we evaluate our actions and thoughts based on what we think is expected.

Sport accentuates self-evaluation due to its public nature and the many opportunities for judgment that it provides. You, first of all, evaluate your performance, and immediate others, such as coaches and teammates, also evaluate it. Then the public, which can include both informed and uninformed viewers, pass judgment on how well you are doing. For high-profile athletes taking part in events with worldwide media coverage, the number of sources of evaluation are mind-boggling. Everyone becomes an expert when evaluating others, and a poor outcome can start a barrage of public criticism.

It is not surprising, therefore, that athletes are often self-critical. Some self-criticism is learned as you progress through the sport, in the form of feedback from others. Such feedback is needed to develop skills, and indeed part of becoming an independent athlete is to take on responsibility for assessing one's own performance. However, the higher an athlete's profile, the more criticism he is apt to receive. And if you don't learn to disregard outside evaluation to a certain extent, you might end up judging yourself too harshly.

Athletes can learn to block out external criticism by ignoring a hostile media and filtering the feedback they receive from others. The toughest critic to block out is usually the voice inside your head, however, the one that knows all too well your most fragile weaknesses and areas for self-doubt. It takes considerable mental discipline to silence that voice. When energy is taken up in worrying about yourself, it is taken away from the performance. Worry often manifests itself as distractibility. Attention wanders from the task, and often in moments of pressure, the self-worrying athlete fails because of a lack of focus that stems simply from insufficient confidence.

How can an athlete forget himself when sport is all about using one's body to its fullest extent? Actually, awareness of the body and its movements is often heightened in flow. It is the awareness of one's ego, or social identity, that recedes into the background. The more attention we invest in the body and its performance, the less is left over to ruminate about saving face or impressing others.

When you are in danger of getting distracted, it helps to be able to focus on the rhythm of your breathing or on the minute changes in the way your muscles feel. Learning to listen to what the body tells you is one of the surest ways to achieve concentration and improve performance.

So, in a paradoxical way, it is often by paying attention to your body that you get to forget the ego! You forget the part of the self that

questions, critiques, and prompts self-doubt. Letting go of this judge frees an athlete to become totally absorbed in the task at hand. More energy is available for the performance, and confidence is not weakened when the ego has no access to attention.

The unselfconscious athlete is not concerned with criticism, real or imagined. There is no worry of failure, no consideration of an unsuccessful outcome and what this might mean in terms of evaluation. These moments of unselfconscious action allow potential to be fully realized, without the limiting influence of worry. Athletes treasure such moments, as they characterize freedom in movement and convey a sense of power.

A skater who was asked what were the important aspects of her flow experiences emphasized the *loss of self-consciousness*, saying that in everything she did in life she was always self-conscious; to experience moments of freedom from such worry was very important. For this athlete, self-consciousness evidenced itself in a lack of confidence, and she recognized that in her sport, showing any signs of lack of confidence would come through readily to others, including the judges of her performance. Flow experiences help to build confidence, demonstrating to the athlete what is possible when the restricting effect of self-consciousness is released.

Let Your Competitors Worry About Themselves

Another source of distraction for athletes is the opposition. Worrying about what a competitor is likely to do and how one's skills will stack up against the opponent prevents absorption in one's own performance, because at least some attention is diverted to the competitor. Of course, part of the task in some sports involves paying close attention to what others are doing. In a middle-distance track race it is necessary to watch other runners so as to keep abreast of any surges and, at an even simpler level, just to keep from tripping. In most team sports, playing successfully means being able to make moves and react to those of the opponents with quick responses. Such attention belongs with task demands and is necessary for optimal performance.

It is the worry about how well one is doing in relation to one's competitors, the comparisons of self to others, that signals inefficient attention. We cannot control what others do; we can only be in charge of our own performance. But our actions of course influence what a competitor can do, and this is all part of strategy in games where there can only be one winner. And then our moves are likely to be countered again by a strong opponent, and so the struggle for supremacy continues. Even when you are knowledgeable of how your opponent reacts, you have no control over what her reaction will be in any particular situation.

Getting caught up in an opponent's play takes away attention from your performance, and unexpected or undesired reactions can distract and upset you. In this way, a competitor you are trying to control can end up controlling you. Learning to separate the ego from your competitors' actions and what these may mean in terms of outcome is an important skill that frees up energy to use for your own performance.

Accept the Environment as a Given

Sport is played in a number of different and non-optimal environments, and each one has the potential to either facilitate or wreak havoc on an athlete's experience. Indoor settings generally have fewer environmental factors at play, but the type of surface, the temperature and humidity, and even the physical attractiveness of these settings can influence athletes' quality of experience. Outdoors, athletes are at the mercy of the weather, and temperature, wind, or humidity can have a large effect on an athlete's performance. The surface is likely to be inconsistent. Rhythm and momentum can be disrupted by changing conditions.

In addition to the physical environment, a myriad of social factors can create an environment of their own. The presence or absence of spectators creates an impact that has potential to distract; family and friends create additional expectations in the mind of the athlete. Add in the interactions between teammates and between athlete and coach, all factors influencing the social setting of performance. On top of the sheer presence of others is the potential influence of recent events that replay in athletes' minds and can drain energy or attention. Furthermore, add the feedback and information others give to athletes before and during performance, and the list of potential sources of worry from the environment escalates. Moreover, umpires and referees can cause worry or other negative emotions. Yes, there are countless things to worry about if you're willing to let them bother you. They can all keep you from tuning in to the experience, let alone becoming absorbed in flow. In one study of elite athletes, over 70 percent of the disruptions to flow that respondents reported were attributed to non-optimal environmental or situational influences, and most of these were perceived to be outside the athletes' control.

By its very nature sport can thus be seen to present many obstacles to total absorption. On the one hand, athletic events provide a clear structure, progression of challenges, and opportunities to achieve goals; these can all be quite amenable to flow. But sport's emphasis on outcomes and winners and its encouragement of self-analysis and self-criticism makes it difficult for athletes to experience the freedom from worry and self-consciousness that are part of flow. Nevertheless, you can rechannel focus and rethink perceptions, and so re-find your CS balance even in unfavorable conditions.

Focus on the Process

Having a process focus means paying attention to the actions, the strategies, and the techniques of performance in your sport. Process is about doing. The opposite of process is outcome, the final results of your doing. We have mentioned how an outcome focus can prevent staying in the present, which is precisely why a process focus is preferable: processes occur in the present, and focusing on them keeps the athlete centered in the performance as it unfolds.

71

It is easier to maintain a process focus when you know clearly what it is you are supposed to do. Having clear goals for all the components of performance ensures you are paying attention to the relevant cues—and only to them. Not getting ahead of yourself is important to maintain a process focus. So while it may be important to plan for subsequent moves or plays, the primary focus should be directed to what is happening in the present moment.

Staying in the moment is a good way to remember what a process focus is all about. When attention is focused on what is going on, you are fully aware of everything affecting your sphere of consciousness. Maintaining this focus means you move forward, staying totally in tune with what is happening. You don't slip behind and worry about past mistakes; nor do you skip ahead to future moves. By staying fully in the present, you center yourself in the performance. You are also in control of your actions and thus able to direct their future.

ONENESS AND THE TRANSFORMATION OF TIME

Among the nine dimensions that we discussed in chapter two, which are all part of the mind-set that induces and characterizes flow, three have special significance: the merging of action and awareness, loss of self-consciousness, and the transformation of time. These three dimensions particularly characterize a state of mind that has become transformed beyond our normal day-to-day experience. Throughout the next chapters we will be using athletes' descriptions to illustrate this special awareness and to demonstrate how it transforms ordinary experience.

As a sense of oneness takes over in the process focus, the distinction blurs between the athlete who is making the movements and the movements themselves. It is in these moments that, to paraphrase Yeats's verse, one can no longer tell the dancer from the dance. When this occurs, the athlete ceases to think of himself as separate from the movements he is making. All one's awareness gets tied up with performing, and when an athlete comes out of this state, he can feel amazed at the distances he's covered or the time that has passed.

A triathlete describing the total absorption she felt in flow mentioned that people would ask how she could stay focused for several hours when competing:

> People are always asking, "How do you keep focused? What do you think about?" Well, there's never any time to think about anything except what you're doing. Even in the Ironman for nine hours . . .

when I'm having a good day I'm not thinking about what I'm going to have when I get home or what I'm going to do. Every single minute you're sort of re-evaluating, "How's this going" and "Are you taking in enough fluids," and so on.

Total focus, or the sense of oneness with what you are doing, manifests itself in different ways, depending on the athlete and her event. A 10k runner who was in flow throughout an entire race explained how a film crew videotaped her for the whole race and yet she was never aware of their presence. Compare this response with that of our cyclist, Simon, who described his awareness as being like a wide-angle lens. The accounts are quite different, but the total attunement with the performance is the same. How athletes process information in flow appears to differ between individuals as well as across sports. Sometimes athletes feel as if they were the only ones left in the world; a person perceives that everyone and everything else becomes absorbed in the athlete's total experience. A figure skater describes the phenomenon well:

Everything else goes away. It almost happens in slow motion, even though you're doing things at the correct time with the music and everything. Nothing else matters; it is just such an eerie, eerie feeling. The audience fades away, except for the brief moment when they were clapping so loudly—actually that was just a part of us. It was all a part of our experience; it never took us out of our focus.

This merging of action and awareness has almost a mystical feeling: it is what Zen monks try to achieve or yogis aim to reach with their meditative practices. Basketball players become one with the ball and with the basket; swimmers are one with the water; cyclists see their bike as an extension of their bodies. Skaters and other performers sense a merging with the music, the audience, the total environment.

Lose Clock Time

The loss of a sense of real time that can occur in deep flow is related to the absorption of attention, which can lead to forgetting the passage of time or to the perception that time is moving at a different speed, compared to normal situations. A runner might check the time on a stopwatch or even a wristwatch at the start and finish of a long run, and be amazed at the discrepancy between what she perceived happened and how much time actually elapsed. Time stops for some athletes in flow; for others, it seems to move more quickly or more slowly than it actually does. Donovan Bailey, 100-meter Olympic champion (and world record holder for this event), is reported as describing the 9.8 seconds it takes him to run the 100 meters as feeling like an eternity, with time seeming to stretch out an incredible amount.

A figure skater describes the sense of control she experienced in flow that made her perceptions of time more fluid:

> Time does quicken and slow; it seems like it almost bends at your will. This is the only time an athlete feels all God-like . . . if it is that through your mind and body you have ultimate control of yourself and through that somehow it seems to change time. For instance, if you're more in focus, [time] will slow down. And if you're feeling really good about something, something really difficult, something that usually takes a long time, [it] goes by very quickly.

The time dimension of flow is one characteristic of total absorption; whereas for some athletes this altered sense or dimension may rarely occur, for others it will be a common characteristic of their totally absorbed flow state.

Does Time Transform for You?

When you are in flow in your sport, do you get a sense of time passing differently from normal, either slowing down or speeding up? Or does it appear to not change at all from the way you usually perceive it? If you have sensed time passing differently, describe what happens in your experience. Then, observe your experience over several days—moments when you are totally absorbed in your performance. What seems to happen? Does time pass differently? In which direction?

Lose the Sense of Effort

Athletes often mention feeling that in flow they are performing automatically. This does not mean that they become machine-like and are devoid of any emotion or awareness. The awareness becomes so complete that the athlete knows moment by moment exactly what to do, and there is no need to reflect upon or question her actions. This can result in feeling like the performance is happening effortlessly by itself. In fact, a great deal of skilled effort is expended but because the athlete is not forcing her actions, it can seem as though the performance is proceeding spontaneously. Such perceptions can be unusual and difficult to describe. A skater illustrates this ambiguity:

It's almost as though you don't have to think. . . . It's like everything goes automatically without [your] thinking. . . . It's like you're on automatic pilot, so you don't have any thoughts; it's kind of strange. And you hear the music, but you're not aware that you're hearing it because it is just kind of a part of it all.

Athletes often remark on another factor of awareness in flow: the ease of movement that accompanies this state. Sport involves varying degrees of physical effort, and all sports lift the level of effort above average. To perform to one's highest levels or surpass existing standards requires a commitment of mental and physical energies to the task. Athletes are pleasantly surprised, when, instead of working harder, they feel they are working more easily to achieve high standards of performance during flow experiences. This runs so counter to what they expect or are used to that it can be difficult to understand or describe. A triathlete attempts to put words to the paradox of performing well with less effort:

It was like I was just floating across the ground, and while it was definitely an effort, it [also] wasn't. . . . You're able to control the effort so much that really in a way it's like it is quite easy, even though you know that you're really putting in. It's not taking out of you as much as it may do in training or in another race. You are going faster, and yet it seems easier. . . . It is hard to describe in words unless you experience it. . . . Just that it is like you know you are working very, very hard, and you're going as fast as you can go, and yet you're doing it quite easily. The two don't go together, but that is how it feels.

Feeling that performance is easy, cruising, putting in a lot less effort—these are characteristics that seem to go contrary to the maxims of "No pain, no gain," "More is better," and "The harder you work at it, the more you will get out of it." Because of the enhanced performance of mind and body in flow, however, performance becomes less of a strain. It seems more like play—which is what sport was supposed to be like in the first place.

THE CLARITY OF FLOW

In the state of flow a clarity of purpose and heightened awareness become one. They can be experienced at different levels or intensities. At one extreme, an activity involving high risk can heighten clarity, as leading solo climber Peter Croft explains:

When you're out soloing a long route, you get into this rhythm that
is beyond exhilarating. . . . You get this super clarity, and you can see
things really, really perfectly.

Soloing, or climbing without ropes, puts the climber in situations of
extreme danger and risk. Few people choose this form of climbing, and
among them Croft is recognized as possessing an extraordinary talent in
this pursuit. His description of the extreme clarity that he finds when he
solos explains in part his ability to be so successful at an activity few
would even contemplate. By not using a rope, Croft is forced to focus his
attention completely on the route he attempts and to keep his mind
clear of any distractions. In turn, he finds soloing seems to lift his mental
acuity to extreme levels, allowing him to see things perfectly and find a
rhythm that provides an optimal experience.

The thrill of a solo rock climber may be a level beyond what most
of us will feel, at least on a regular basis, when participating in sport.
Nonetheless, the clarity of purpose that any sporting activity provides
is usually greater than what we can experience in most mundane everyday activities. All sports have a structure of rules and goals that
allow the mind and body to get involved in a total, harmonious interaction. Knowing how to build on this existing structure by focusing
on ever clearer and more attainable goals makes it more likely and
easier for each of us to get the most enjoyment from sport, as well as
from life as a whole. The next chapter will discuss how and why clear
goals are necessary for flow.

5

Knowing Where You're Going

P sychological well-being requires full involvement of the entire organism; without clear demands on attention, the mind begins to turn toward personal problems. When it seems that there is nothing to do, the mind becomes unfocused, and we can start to feel depressed. Productivity decreases, as energy is not directed in specific and purposeful ways. Sadness and boredom begin to take over consciousness. Most people think that all they need to be happy is to have free time to do in it what they want. But just having free time is not enough: one also needs something to do that will focus the mind.

Flow elevates moods by keeping us from ruminating about the downside of life—it focuses psychic energy on a doable goal, and while we are pursuing it, the concerns of everyday life are temporarily held in abeyance. When in flow, we have a clear sense of what we must do, and these goals direct action in a moment-by-moment fashion.

One of the most important factors for getting into flow is knowing what it is you are trying to achieve. Sport provides clear goals and rules for action, based on the structures that have evolved and serve to define each sport event. No matter what sport you may decide to take up, it will come with its own rules and boundaries that will provide a clear structure for how the activity is to be played. Goals are a key part of this structure. For example, in many field and team sports, the goal is to score points. How points can be scored will be clearly defined—for example, by crossing the opposition's goal line or putting a ball into a goal area.

Many sports have extensive rule books that set out in great detail what the movement possibilities are and how they will be evaluated. In the sport of gymnastics for example, there is a code of points for every skill and its possible variations, each of which has a specific numerical value. When designing a routine, gymnast and coach refer to the code to determine what skills to include so as to reach a certain points-value. It is clear what the goals or objectives are, and this allows for precise focus on the elements of the routine during performance, both by the gymnast and the judges.

One result of such a clearly defined action structure in sport is a freeing up of psychic energy. Once an athlete learns the relevant rules and goals, all of her attention can be focused on doing the task to the best of her ability.

This is one of the reasons why sports are so enjoyable. They are built to provide clear goals and rules, so that we can become involved completely in activities that demand full participation. Sports attract a variety of people with many different motives for being involved. An athlete's goal might be to prepare mentally and physically for breaking a record; a spectator's goal might be to see a great rivalry played out; a coach's goal might be to prepare the team to do its best.

The goals that sports provide also vary through time. Before the event, the athlete focuses on training and rehearsing mentally the coming performance; during the event, goals might change as one adapts to unforeseen conditions; afterward the athlete might revise her goals as a result of what she has learned from the event. Given that sports provide all these opportunities for involvement, it is not surprising that they are one of the most life-enhancing activities humans have devised.

WINNING AS A GOAL OR A GUIDEPOST

Many coaches and athletes believe that the only goal worth striving for is winning. There is no question that competition is at the essence of sports. The reason goals are so clear in sports is that the objective is to run the fastest race, score the most goals, jump the highest, throw the javelin or the discus farthest. Everyone can see and evaluate the performance. Victory is the crowning moment of a dramatic performance that has been full of unpredictability and tension. The winner is elated, and the spectators vicariously share in the resolution of the staged conflict. Without competition it would be easy to lose concentration, to become distracted or uninvolved—to fall out of flow.

On the other hand, if the only goal of the athlete is to win, flow is also endangered. If your attention is focused exclusively on winning, you cannot pay attention to what is happening at the moment. You don't notice the speed of your stride, the rate of your breathing, or what your opponents are doing. You become anxious, and in the effort to achieve the only reward that counts for you—victory—you miss the opportunity to enjoy the rewards that come from a move well executed or a play well made, or simply from feeling the body doing its best in a difficult effort.

The Double-Edged Sword

Competition can be a powerful motivator to performance, creating high challenge. In this light, competition is conducive to flow. There is a competitive element within most individuals, and sport generally brings this motivation to life. Competition provides an opportunity to test your skills in an objectively evaluated domain; through taking part in competition, feedback about your skills is provided.

Competition can, however, be a double-edged sword so far as achieving flow is concerned. What is valued and devalued in the competitive process holds the key to the impact of competition on the sport experience. When winning and outperforming others becomes paramount, the process of experiencing becomes lost and the road to flow becomes more arduous.

Road Map to the Competition

It is useful to remember that the word *competition* came from the two Latin words *con petire*, which meant "to search together." The idea was that the best way to find out how good your skills were was to match them against the skills of another person. The point of competition was not to beat someone else, but to search out the best in yourself.

The fact that sport has evolved historically so as to provide clear goals does not mean that one automatically discovers what has to be done just by participating in a sport. While a sport provides a road map for performance, that map must be internalized by the athlete so that it can provide direction at such a personal level that it becomes spontaneous and automatic. But the first step is to map clear goals.

KEYS TO YOUR GAME PLAN

When elite athletes are asked what keeps them from experiencing flow, they frequently mention not being physically prepared or ready for the event. This includes factors such as deficits in physical conditioning, not feeling good physically, problems with food or fluid intake, fatigue, and injury.

Condition Yourself

If an athlete knows she has not done the necessary training to be in good shape for an event, flow is unlikely to occur. On the other hand, being fatigued from too heavy a training load is also recognized as a factor preventing flow. Finding a balance between too much and too little training is essential for both athletes and coaches. A triathlete explains the problem:

> Fatigue from the previous days' training. . . . Training load as much as anything prevents you from getting there [to flow], but it is a Catch-22, because the only way you can get to that state is to have a heavy training load.

Flow may not be equally easy to achieve through all the stages of a season, especially when training is periodized, due to the workloads that athletes carry when heavy conditioning is required. On the other hand, lacking good physical condition, athletes may not be able to perform physically to the levels necessary for their skills to be extended, again making flow unlikely. When physical preparation is not at optimal levels, athletes are often less certain of what they will be able to do when performing. This uncertainty creates a lack of clarity in goals, which makes flow more difficult to achieve.

Sometimes athletes are well prepared physically but fail in other aspects of precompetitive preparation. What they do immediately before competition might be poorly organized, or they might not have set aside enough time to be mentally or strategically ready for the event ahead. Being unprepared can be a big stumbling block, as is clear in this runner's comment about the consequences of not having made a race plan:

> If you stand up on the block and just expect it to happen, and haven't thought about what you want to think about, it won't happen.

Know Your Goals

When an athlete does not have any goals, or when the goals are not believed in or valued, there will be little motivation for doing the activity. Without motivation there is little energy or impetus to seek challenge. The nervousness one feels before an important event is a clear signal of being motivated to do well. When lacking motivation, an athlete may feel too relaxed and find it difficult to harness the energy required for optimal performance. If the motivation is low, relaxation may turn into anxiety or worry—the realization that it is difficult to perform well without a certain amount of energy that nerves can provide before an event.

What is an athlete trying to achieve when he competes in a sport event? Preparing to compete, an athlete will likely have in mind a purpose he would like to accomplish. These achievement goals are often one of two types: task goals or outcome goals. An athlete with a *task goal* desires to improve his or her own performance in a certain way and is not concerned with how the performance may compare with other participants' achievements. Task-oriented athletes enjoy the process of competition and the challenge of extending personal limits.

An athlete with an *outcome* or ego goal, on the other hand, sets standards in comparison to other competitors, and is focused on how well he can do against others of similar ability. Final results are what matters to the ego-oriented athlete, and success is judged on outperforming competitors.

To illustrate, a runner lining up for a race may have predetermined splits and an overall time goal she wants to meet, based on her times over previous races at this distance. These are task goals, for they relate to the individual's previous standards and the amount of personal improvement being targeted. On the other hand, the runner may set a goal of finishing in the top five, an outcome goal. Of course, a runner may set both time and place goals, combining task and outcome goals. It is what the athlete is focused on during the event that becomes critical to the achievement of flow. A task goal allows the runner to focus on her own race and not constantly compare herself with the other competitors. Furthermore, a task orientation is much more within the athlete's control. The runner can set times based on recent past performances and her present condition. The challenge can thus be set at an appropriate level, facilitating the athlete's being able to find her own CS balance. Compare this to a goal of placing in a certain position. This is much less within an individual's control, as it depends on how every other runner performs on this particular occasion. The challenge thus becomes much more fluid and apt to change, depending on the circumstances of the race.

Competition is an opportunity to test one's skills against others, and by definition competition involves comparison of performance to others. Outcome goals are not bad goals for athletes to have, and many competitive athletes will have both task and outcome goals. When an athlete strongly believes in her ability, outcome goals can be very motivating and challenging.

Task goals can always provide opportunities for challenge if they are set just above an athlete's present skill level, regardless of what that level is. When goals are targeted at constantly taking an individual's performance to the next level, challenge is always present. Athletes who have won Olympic gold medals and world championships continue to motivate themselves to perform to higher and higher levels by focusing on trying to take their performance up a notch or by creating new types of challenges within their sport. Thus, a highly successful athlete may change events—or the change may even be to a completely different sport. Michael Jordan, who had achieved so much within the game of basketball, found himself looking to a new sport after three NBA championship rings. Not finding what he was looking for in baseball, he decided to return to basketball and set himself new challenges, which kept his motivation alive, his skills improving, and success continuing to come his way.

Set Clear and Specific Goals

When motivation is lacking, preparation for an event is often compromised. Going into an event low in motivation or without any goals rarely leads to flow. This type of situation occurs when you see no challenge ahead or, conversely, when the challenges seem too high. In either case, motivation and goal setting in turn suffer. Either the situation is perceived as low in importance and not worth investing mental or physical effort in or the challenge is perceived so unlikely to be attained that, again, effort is withheld. A figure skater explains how problems with motivation prevent flow: "It's really hard to get into that state because you can talk to yourself, but if it's not believed 100 percent and thought of, needed, and desired, then you don't get it."

Having the necessary motivation is usually not a problem for dedicated athletes, although there will be times when even the most intense participants will experience lapses in motivation. Goals are the building blocks of motivation, and learning to set the right goal helps immensely in maintaining your intent at appropriate levels.

Setting goals seems on the surface to be a simple task. However, there is skill involved in making goals work for you. Poor goal setting can be just as bad as—or even worse than—having no goals at all. Suppose a swimmer, for example, sets a goal of swimming the 200-meter freestyle in under two minutes, but this goal is clearly beyond his present skill levels. During the race, the swimmer finds himself way back in the field and not on target with his splits. The negative mental state this leads to can take the swimmer further from the reaches of flow than if he had dived into the pool without any goals at all and just swum the race.

Goals that are not realistic can decrease motivation, because failure takes away from enthusiasm and self-confidence. It is both an art and a science to set goals at just the right level of difficulty. A basic principle is to set goals just above one's current level of performance. This should provide incentive and motivate the athlete to reach a bit further than the last time, while not overwhelming self-confidence by setting the goal too high.

"Do-your-best" goals are also usually unproductive, as they do not direct attention to the specific aspects of performance one needs to focus on. We hear examples of general goals all the time: "Just go out there and do your best," " I am going to do all I can," and "Give it 100 percent." Such slogans and advice might enhance motivation, but they do not provide goals. To direct action effectively, a goal has to be specific. These example statements do not address what specific actions are to be taken. Learning to set goals that work for you and not against you requires time and guidance. It is well worth the investment, however, as the right type of goal is one of the keys to flow.

Goals that are specific and task-focused give direction to action. Splits, points of focus, technique, and strategic plans can easily be converted into specific goals that provide a guideline for performance. Stating what you want to do in terms of specific actions turns general ideas into goals. Doing this for the major components of performance provides a road map to direct actions throughout the event. Writing goals down helps to make them clear and specific and provides a point for feedback and evaluation as performance is tested against the standards you set. Visualizing the event beforehand, focusing on key elements of the performance as if viewing them on a video screen, helps many athletes make their goals real and their performance more effortless.

What are your specific goals? What goals do you currently have for your sport performance? Think of what challenges you are facing in relation to your sport and what you are trying to achieve. Put these in the first column in table 5.1, followed in column 2 by the specific actions you need to follow to meet these challenges. Turn these into goal statements in column 3. A brief example is given at the top of the table.

Make Goals Automatic

Making goals concrete and rehearsing them well allows a individual to act on them automatically. A well-learned routine that is designed to bring the athlete to her best focus and optimal arousal level as the time to compete draws near, one based on predetermined goals for focus and activation, sets the stage for optimal experience. The performance road map begins as a rough draft, and it requires constant attention to its details in the formative stages. Once clearly defined, the next step is to learn to internalize the directions.

Internalizing the directions is like driving a car to a new destination: you need a clear and detailed map, and during the first journey you may refer to the map many times to ensure finding the destination. Once

Table 5.1		
Your Specific Goals		
Current challenges	*Specific actions*	*Goals*
Make qualifying time	Speed training	Two speed sessions per week
	Mental race plan	Develop and practice race plan

you've made a few trips and defined the checkpoints, the map does not need to be referred to except if you lose the way. In the early stages of your sport or a particular event the "road map" will need to be followed closely and performance monitored according to the directions the map provided. Once you've learned the way, however, a mental picture is formed of what needs to be done, and you are free to immerse yourself in the athletic performance at an automatic level.

Making one's performance automatic does not mean turning into a preprogrammed robot. After the competition starts, many unanticipated conditions might arise, requiring changes in the prepared scenario. A gymnast, for example, might notice stiffness in some muscles, suggesting a slight alteration in the prepared routine; a runner might realize that the one competitor he had planned to pace behind is running too slowly, so he chooses a different target. Only by paying undivided attention to the performance can the athlete choose the best course of action, and sometimes that even means improvising a new goal. It is not easy to perfect an automatic performance and at the same time keep one's options open in case changes are called for. But it is just this combination that makes effortless flow possible.

Enhance Your Motivation

Just as motivation is aided by setting goals, the power of goals increases when there is high motivation to achieve them. Placing importance on the event energizes and focuses attention, as this hockey player comments: "The more important I perceive it, the higher the pressure, the better I perform. More in flow—you become so single-minded."

When you clearly know what you want and are determined to reach it, you are lifting both challenge and skill to flow levels. The goals harness psychic energy and direct it toward the desired outcome. High levels of motivation translate into determination to reach the goals. And this focus not only improves the quality of experience, but it often also leads to unexpected achievements. Many outstanding sporting performances have resulted when determination drove the athlete to previously unattainable heights. The breaking of the four-minute mile, the ascents of the world's highest peaks, claiming of titles by so-called underdogs have come about from the combination of outstanding athletic talent with unshakable determination to achieve the set goal.

Power of Determination

Roger Bannister, the first man to run the mile in under four minutes, had this to say about the power of determination:

> The human spirit is indomitable. No one can say you must not run faster than this or jump higher than that. There will never be a time when the human spirit will not be able to better existing world marks. Man is capable of running the mile in three-and-a-half minutes.

Enjoy Optimal Readiness

Being in great physical shape gives a mental as well as a physical edge to performance. Knowing you have put in the hard work and trained well increases the chances of performing physically at optimal levels.

It also generates confidence, another important flow facilitator. A rower describes how good training helps readiness:

> If it's going well in training, you get confidence from that and can approach your race in a confident state—confident that you've done it all before and you can do it now.

Getting to the point of optimal physical readiness involves having done the training, being in good physical shape, being well hydrated and having followed an appropriate diet, being rested, and having tapered or peaked for the performance. A triathlete describes how he needs to feel that he deserves to be doing well in order to experience flow:

> In order to go well you have to know you *deserve* to go well. You have to know it's a race you've set as a goal. You've got to know that you've trained properly for it and you deserve to be going well in that race. Then if you do start to go well, you get a spontaneous sort of spiral; when you're going into flow, then you'll know that's where you deserve to be.

Optimal Physical Readiness. Although the focus of this book is the psychological factors for optimal states, sport is by definition a physical encounter, and attention to the physical factors for optimal readiness is critically important. Sports vary in their physical demands, of course, and the factors that are important for optimal readiness vary according to what the sport demands. The factor of hydration may not be critical in all sports, but in some it is vital that an athlete going into an event should drink an adequate amount of liquid. Here is how a rower describes the effects of good hydration:

> How hydrated you are . . . like if your nerves are zinging, you can feel when your nerves are sensitive and really open: your outside receptors are working really well. And if you're not hydrated enough, the receptors aren't working well; you don't start to sweat easily, and your motivation won't be crisp.

Notice the interconnectedness between the physical and mental components of readiness. The rower describes how the level of liquids in the body influences nerve impulses and alertness, drawing a direct parallel between having taken in sufficient fluids and motivation during performance. Not all athletes experience such dramatic effects from fluid intake, but the important point is that physical and mental factors reciprocally influence each other.

Optimal Mental Readiness. Understanding optimal mental readiness is more elusive than knowing the optimal physical conditions for an athlete, because mental factors are much more difficult to observe and measure objectively. How do we know when we have just the right level of motivation or concentration? Optimal readiness is an individual matter, as each person requires a slightly different package of factors. Individuals vary, for example, in how aroused or relaxed they like to feel going into performance. There is considerable variation even on the physical side, with athletes having different schedules for tapering, warming up, and taking in food and fluid prior to performance. Nevertheless, the mental factors are still more individualized.

Achieving optimal mental readiness for any particular person requires two main steps. The first consists of paying close attention to what happens before and during performance. If necessary, this might involve taking notes, keeping a personal record, and going over things with a coach or teammate. The second step is applying the conditions that were present in performances that successfully produced flow to future performances. This might involve a process of trial and error, of making adjustments and gradually becoming more aware of both the target state and the factors and processes for getting there. For example, some athletes feel that wearing a particular uniform or driving to the stadium by a particular route allows them to concentrate better. Although such behavior is sometimes dismissed as superstition, familiar stimuli often do facilitate immersion in the activity and help to bring about flow.

Prepare for Competitions

Part of optimal preparation includes the thoughts and actions prior to performance. The time horizon of preparation can be extremely broad. For instance, a gymnast might develop the goal of making the Olympic team four years hence. At the same time, she might have goals for regional and national trials coming up in one or two years. Then there are shorter-term goals spanning weeks, days, or even hours ahead.

Precompetitive plans and preparation are important flow facilitators. Having a routine and following it on the day of competition is a great way to ensure mental and physical readiness when it comes time to start performing. Athletes vary in how they like to ready themselves for competition. For instance, some people feel more relaxed when they are surrounded by others before an event; others prefer to collect their thoughts by being alone before competing. Although one sometimes cannot be isolated physically, it is still possible in that event to focus inwardly, as Simon explains:

Even if I'm not in a room by myself, it's just like thought collection. I might be standing in the middle of the bunch waiting for the start gun to go off, but I must turn inward.

Following specific routines, including mental preparation, allows you to feel ready and to have a clear idea of what you are going to do in the event. Some athletes see having a specific race or event plan as critical. A race plan can free the athlete from worry about competitors:

With my race plans now, I've thought about every possible thing that can happen . . . so there's no ifs or buts or whats. You're still a bit worried about what other people are doing if you don't have a race plan.

Knowing everything is in place allows Simon to focus on the task and to switch into the automatic functioning of the flow process. A javelin thrower also describes the feeling that accompanies total preparation:

The fact that I've done everything possible on my physical and mental side, that every facet is covered—that reassures my conscious mind that I've done everything. Then I just have to let myself switch off and let it happen.

Mental plans for competition are discussed in more detail in chapter 7. Being *well-prepared* physically and mentally and totally *ready* in mind and body for the performance gives both an edge and a sense of confidence. You can forget the usual worries and instead have total involvement in the process. Goals set in advance direct preparation and help ensure readiness. Goals for the time immediately before, as well as during, performance direct attention and ensure that a clear sense of purpose accompanies your actions. Both types of goals, for the long and the short term, are essential for reaching flow.

chapter

6

Taking Advantage of Feedback

When you know how well you are doing, when feedback is clear and immediate, you feel more alive and your mood perks up. Having clear goals helps to improve experience, but alone it is not enough. Another important ingredient is to feel, moment by moment, that you are on the way toward reaching those goals. Psychologists who study happiness find that people who only set themselves long-term goals (such as making a million dollars 20 years hence or retiring to Florida when they turn 65) are in general less happy than people who set goals that can be reached next month, next year—or later the same day.

The reason that setting sights on the end of a long journey is less satisfying than having a shorter-term goal is that it is difficult to tell whether you are making any headway. Rather, it is easy to get discouraged or distracted along the way. Whereas if you break up the journey into smaller stages, aiming only to reach the next one, then each step brings you *noticeably* closer to where you intend to go; this keeps you attentive and involved in the task.

93

FILTERING FEEDBACK

For flow to occur, it is not necessary for the feedback you receive to always be positive. If you lose your way on a hike in the woods, you are not getting closer to your goal; yet because you have a goal, you know that you have to get back on the trail, and that knowledge keeps you alert and searching. Getting lost on a purposeful journey is more likely to produce flow than a safe but aimless wandering.

Sport contains many possibilities for feedback. Because of the clearly defined challenges in sport, athletes know when they are doing well or poorly by evaluating their performance in relation to the task demands and their own goals for performance. Task demands are the built-in characteristics of the activity that define successful outcomes. For example, many sports involve a target of some sort that must be reached. In basketball it is scoring baskets; in archery, hitting the mark; in soccer, getting the ball into the net. Achieving the goals of the sport activity leads to positive feedback regarding performance.

An athlete's own goals also provide opportunities for monitoring progress. These goals might range from improving a personal record time in a race to simply finishing the race. You might strive to accomplish the same goal but with less effort and more grace or you might go after perfecting a single element in a complex performance. The more diverse the goals, the more opportunities there are for immersing yourself in the activity—and for enjoying it. And other things being equal, the more flow one derives from sport, the more effortless and successful the performance is likely to be.

> If you set a goal for yourself and are able to achieve it, you have won your race. Your goal can be to come in first, to improve your performance, or just to finish the race—it's up to you.
>
> —Dave Scott, five-time Hawaii Ironman champion

Kinesthetic Awareness

It is not necessary to score a goal or win a game to know how your performance is going. The feedback from the movements of the body allows you to make ongoing adjustments to keep on track or to get back on it. Known as *kinesthetic awareness*, this feel for one's performance is a key component of feedback systems in sport. Kinesthetic awareness lets a gymnast know where he is in space during aerial moves; it provides a golfer with a sense of whether the club head is in

© Mary Langenfeld Photo

the right direction in the various phases of the swing. The rebounder in basketball knows exactly when to jump and reach for the ball, and in countless other examples, kinesthetic awareness provides the internal information an athlete needs to optimize her movements. Athletes are coached to use as many relevant senses as they can, but for the correctness in their movements none is more critical than the sense of feel.

Outcome Information

In addition to having an internal source of feedback, athletes encounter many other forms of information about their performance. The outcomes of movements provide immediate feedback about how successful the moves were, allowing individuals to know whether actions were correct or in need of adjustment. Outcomes may be large-scale, such as a goal scored or a foul awarded. Outcomes may also be small in scope, such as a mistimed swing or a change in a breathing pattern.

In most athletic settings, of course, it is not only the athlete who is aware of the success or failure of his activities. Some of the enjoyment in watching sports hinges on anticipating what might happen on the field, and then seeing whether things turned out the way one expected. Spectators who can appreciate the fine points of a game are able to lose themselves in the action almost as much as the athletes who compete. Sport is a public domain, and performance is evaluated in a very public way.

Teammates, opponents, coaches, and spectators can all provide feedback to let an athlete know whether she is on course. Sometimes this feedback is unwanted and may be ignored, but when it is helpful, athletes can benefit from taking in the information that others involved in the situation provide.

We have discussed some of the sources of feedback that sport provides the performer. Table 6.1 lists these sources in its first column. In the second column, there's space for you to place an example from your sport. You can also write in additional sources at the bottom of the table.

KEYS TO USING FEEDBACK EFFECTIVELY

Athletes are seemingly surrounded with possibilities for feedback. Sometimes they become anxious during performance, daunted by the sheer volume of feedback. They're unsure whether they are doing enough or too much.

If you have found yourself in this uncertain state, you can learn to harness the potential of relevant information by first analyzing how you have been using it.

Avoid the Sidetracks

Because sport provides so much sensory stimulation, getting distracted by unhelpful or irrelevant information is a real possibility. Opponents may do their best to frustrate you. Weather conditions can make con-

Table 6.1

Sources of Feedback for Athletes

Source of feedback	Example from your sport
Kinesthetic awareness	
Coach information	
Teammate information	
Opposition information	
Spectator information	
Outcome information	
Feel for correct skill execution	
Changes in momentum	
Additional sources:	

centration more difficult. Perhaps the crowd, by its presence and response, makes you more aware of errors and shortcomings. For example, home-team fans might try their best to upset the focus of the visiting team. It takes disciplined attention not to get sidetracked by unwanted or negative information during performance.

Sometimes it is uncontrollable events, like getting a flat tire during a bike race or tripping in a hole while you're running, that can really trip one up mentally. Often it is an athlete's own self-consciousness that creates disruption. Carrying outside stresses into the event or becoming emotionally upset during the course of performance can distort perceptions and awareness and make flow difficult. Here is how one athlete describes the negative effect of her emotions on performance:

> Emotions tend to interfere with it—your feelings about people, places. . . . If you consider how you will feel after it's over, you go right off the end. . . . Emotions are something that is really powerful; they can stuff you up and force you out of that state.

This athlete found herself getting distracted by thoughts about people and about the outcome and how they would make her feel. Such information is still feedback of a sort, but it is irrelevant to the task at hand; it disrupts flow and detracts from performance.

It is easy to become sidetracked when there are many stimuli clamoring for attention. When information is also emotion-laden, it can make someone forget his present goal; instead of concentrating on the race, he starts worrying about what the coach or teammates will say in the locker room. Coaches also have to discipline themselves, as athletes do, not to become sidetracked when the team's performance is going poorly, when referees seem to be unfairly penalizing one's athletes, or when one of the many unpredictable and unsettling events of sport competition occur.

Keep Negative Feedback in Its Place

It is difficult to keep a positive attitude in the face of criticism or negative feedback. Negatives sometimes seem to carry more power than positive feedback, and just one piece of information that says you are not doing well can wipe out previous evidence of success. It is easy to lose confidence by focusing on errors and *perceiving* that you are failing.

What should you do when it seems that things are not going well? It is impossible to be involved in sport—or anything else in life—without experiencing failure again and again. As Michael Jordan says in a promotional advertisement, "I've failed over and over again in my life, and that is why I succeed." Considering the level of success that Jordan has achieved, such a statement might at first appear unbelievable. But to achieve success in any endeavor requires taking risks, stepping from the known to the unknown, and facing defeat many times over. Jordan's level of success could not have come about without his having overcome setbacks, disappointments, failures. This quote by Jordan is also a reminder that challenge is the key to successful experiences: failure can be a tremendous motivator for success.

Depending on how you interpret negative feedback, the information can either hurt or help in the long run. Sometimes a bad start in a race or a match can spell the end of the whole event, as this rugby player comments: "I've never been in a sense of flow when we've got off to a bad start. If you start badly, you just go downhill." With a rugby game lasting 80 minutes, however, a response like this can mean a poor start will lead to a long and painful game!

Does it have to be the case that a bad start will wash out the rest of the event? Do small errors during the event mean the whole performance is going to suffer? Sometimes the precision and timing of sport events makes even the smallest of errors consequential, but how the mind reacts is at least as important as the actual error itself. When competing in track cycling, Simon explains, the smallest of out-placed movements might affect his race, but he also recognizes that his mind plays an important role in what eventuates:

> I mean really small—like you might look at a different place on the track or you might move the handlebars just like that a bit, and it'll put you off. Really, really little things! Wish my mind wouldn't work that fast. I think it's a case of where the mind is trying to do so well that it overcompensates on everything in a way.

If wanting to do well becomes too strong a goal in the athlete's mind, instead of the goal's facilitating flow, it may disrupt the rhythm or timing of movements. Balancing the desire to do well with the need for precision and for automatic reactions can present a challenge in sports where exactness of movements and timing play critical roles.

Staying focused in the face of negative feedback is a difficult challenge. It is hard to stay positive when you see competitors pulling ahead of you or when you make a mistake. Sometimes the negative feedback comes from teammates and problems with the interactions among team members.

Interact With Teammates

Athletes mention a lack of synergy in the team as a factor that often prevents them from reaching an optimal experience. A pursuit cyclist saw as a major deterrent that the team's pace was not smooth:

> If things aren't going smoothly, that would prevent it [flow] because I think things have to be going smoothly. The pace—if someone upsets the nice smoothness of it, it upsets your rhythm, upsets your focus.

Some sports rely on the successful interaction between team members for optimal performance. Certainly in an event like teams pursuit, if one cyclist is out of rhythm or unable to keep pace, the whole team suffers. In pairs figure skating, for example, success is defined by how well the pair can skate as a unit. One skater may be in flow one minute and the next find herself flat on the ice due to her partner having erred. Here is how one pairs skater describes the effect of an error on the ice:

> If you miss a handhold, or somebody trips unexpectedly, you could trip and fall just gliding forward, on no difficulty. When something like that happens, it's like a bomb went off!

Obviously, having to connect with others' performances as well as your own presents an entirely new set of challenges to team athletes. Achieving the CS balance that leads to flow becomes dependent to some extent on how successfully the team can interconnect, both in terms of performance and emotional relationships. Team athletes mention both factors as influencing flow. So, in addition to the problems posed by performance itself, negative team talk and negative feelings among team members will force attention away from the goals of the activity, and disrupt the experience.

When performance involves two or more athletes working together, the congruence of teammates' goals will influence the quality of feedback and, in turn, the quality of experience during the event. In figure skating it is essential that both partners reach for the same goal at the same time. A pairs-skater discusses how important partner unity is to his achieving flow:

> Unity is absolutely critical. Because without it, I don't care how fabulous I was feeling. If my partner was tripping all over the ice, I had a failure going as far as I was concerned. . . . Working well with my partner, on the other hand, was just a really, really, really relaxed oneness, a sameness with my partner and with the ice surface and with the audience and the surroundings.

The difference that unity made in this pair's skating illustrates how critical teamwork is to the experience of flow. In team situations, a sense of unity among team members provides the positive feedback that helps lift the event to high levels of performance and a flow experience.

Open Communication

Communication between teammates provides information about performance and relationships, and both are important parts of the feedback system. When performance depends on interacting with teammates, communication difficulties can seriously upset outcomes.

Comments that are task-focused and positive help the whole team. Outcome-focused feedback or derogatory statements, in contrast, can be detrimental to the team's performance and ability to achieve flow. So what team members and coaches say in the locker room at half-time can either turn a poor performance around or make likely the slide's continuing into the second half.

Coaches are a powerful source of communication for athletes; what a coach says and how he says it can impact an athlete's focus and confidence. Part of being a successful coach is being able to provide the kind of information that will allow athletes to enter and stay in the flow state. There are many different coaching styles and methods of conveying information. When there is a bad match between the communication style of a coach and the needs of her athletes, breakdowns in interactions occur—often because of mismatched goals and expectations. An athlete whose coach gives more information in the field than she can absorb will block out the content of the coach's words, and she will be unable to receive the helpful feedback a coach's eye is trained to pick up. Conversely, a coach who is stone-faced and imparts very little information does not provide a key source of feedback that might benefit athletes during performance.

The signals that the body provides during performance are one line of communication. Another is what happens among teammates and between athlete and coach. If the feedback an individual gets from these sources is useful in achieving flow, it is in the athlete's interest to be as open to it as possible. But if the information someone gets interferes with concentration on the task, the person should learn to ignore or screen it out.

Open lines of communication between coaches and athletes and among team members are important ingredients for successful performance. They are also key for finding flow, particularly when an individual's performance depends on these interactions. Trust between players, a positive team feeling, unison of movements, and focus among interacting teammates can all influence whether one or all the team members are in flow during performance.

The influence of communications begins well before the onset of the event. What is said—and not said—during warm-up or in a pre-game meeting can affect the athletes throughout the event. The content and intent, along with how the information is perceived, all determine the potential for positive or negative impact. Once the event has begun, information given by the coach, as well as feedback among team members, influences individuals' and team psyches. A rower explains how he and his coach communicated when the rower was on the water:

> I look at my coach and give him a nod, and he immediately knows; the boat's humming along and he can, from outside, detect minute changes in the boat speed. It is incredible how minute a change he can detect, and what I try and do is reinforce him, reinforce his feedback ability by giving a nod when I know it's going well. So over a period of time he's got a lot of these nods so that he knows it's going well. And when it's not going well, we can immediately regain focus or stop, rest, start again.

The setting of rules for how and what information is communicated during an event, based on knowing what is helpful to both the team as a whole and to each individual, can help ensure that the impact of the feedback is positive. In the final analysis, however, it is what an individual decides to do with incoming information that has the biggest influence on his or her state of mind.

That is why filtering feedback, based on what is helpful and unhelpful information for performance, is an important skill to develop. The kind of feedback that it is important to listen to provides information about how well you are progressing toward your goals. Table 6.2 is designed to help you get into the practice of linking your feedback sources to your goals to facilitate flow. For each entry, write short-term goals you are currently working toward in the first column. In the second column, write down sources of feedback that you can use to evaluate your progress toward these goals. Learning to filter feedback and make adjustments in a smooth and nonevaluative manner are important skills for athletes and coaches wanting to experience flow.

Focus on Your Own Performance

Feedback is neither good nor bad in itself. It is simply information that can be used to monitor and adjust performance as needed. There is a tendency in sport to focus exclusively on those signs that tells us how close we are to winning—for instance, by keeping the eyes fixed on the scoreboard. Such information can indeed be useful because it tells you how well your skills are meeting the demands of the situation. When you perceive opportunity to improve within the event, knowing you are losing can lead to extra effort and a lifting of your game.

Watching professional sport provides illustrations of how skilled and disciplined athletes can use feedback about unsuccessful performance

Table 6.2	
Feedback Linked to Goals	
Goal	*Feedback*
Make qualifying time.	
• Speed training (two sessions per week)	• Feeling of speed and rhythm during sprints
• Practice mental race plan	• Monitor progress through steps of plan, as I implement plan in practice.

and turn their game around. For example, in the 1996 U.S. Basketball Conference Finals, Michael Jordan had shot 2 for 21 in the first three quarters of a game. He came back to make 20 points in the fourth. Jordan didn't need to know his statistics to tell that his game was off. The trajectory of the ball, the missed timing, and the other cues Jordan has learned to pay attention to would have told him he needed to do something differently. He demonstrated exceptional ability to read the game, take in useful information about his performance, and turn things around on many occasions.

Sometimes it is very difficult to increase the level of skills during the event, particularly when you perceive them already to be stretched to the limit. In these instances, try redefining the challenges to help yourself find your CS balance and return to flow. Instead of focusing on a lack of skills and losing heart, it makes more sense to go for a lesser but doable goal: perhaps to contain the loss, end with a flourish, or even save one's energy for the next event. That is why a person who recognizes multiple challenges, or goals that go beyond the simple outcome, is much more likely to experience flow.

You can often recapture optimal experience by defining challenges in terms of your own possibilities and then monitoring performance as it progresses during the event, based on the feedback about how you are using your skills. It is a much more productive way to develop potential than by riveting your attention on victory and defeat.

Be Self-Aware

Often all it takes to open the door to flow is either increasing skills or lowering the challenges in a particular situation. But neither will happen unless you are self-aware, able to quickly recognize when there is an imbalance and use the feedback to make adjustments to skills, or to goals, depending on the opportunities in the situation.

It may surprise you to read that it's okay to be self-aware. Perhaps you're guessing that self-awareness is detrimental to flow—and certainly not a particularly personable character trait to have. It may even seem paradoxical that merging with action leaves room for self-awareness. Self-awareness simply means paying attention to the cues provided by movements and reactions, and making adjustments to what you are doing when something is not quite right. Without self-awareness an athlete misses important cues that can lead to a positive change in performance.

It is important to distinguish between self-awareness and what we have previously described as self-*consciousness*. The two terms can be easily confused, even though they describe different states of mind. To be self-conscious means that we look at ourselves from the outside, as it were, and worry about how we are doing, how we look to others. Self-consciousness interferes with flow and endangers performance because our attention is split between doing what we have to do and watching ourselves doing it.

When we are self-aware, however, we don't think about the self at all; we just process information about the fine nuances of our involvement in the activity. Athletes often have better self-awareness than nonathletes do, because they need to continually monitor their body during sport. A figure skater describes how it feels when things are going really well:

> When it was good, I knew every single moment; in fact I even remember going down into a jump and, this is awful but, thinking, "Oh gosh! This is so real! I'm so clear in my thoughts. . . . "I felt in such control of everything, of every little movement. I was very aware, you know like what was on my hand, I could feel my rings, I could feel everything, and I felt like I had control of anything.

Self-aware athletes learn to listen to their bodies and to know what good performance feels like. Having a good sense for how movements feel means that an athlete can also make good use of imagery, or mental practice. Imagery is an important mental skill for practicing discrete movements and visualizing desired outcomes. But to successfully visualize moves, an athlete must know how it feels to execute them in real life, and to do so she must pay attention to her performance. Only then can she practice mentally just as if she were physically performing the movements.

Self-awareness can even rescue athletes from imminent danger. Solo climber Peter Croft, renowned for taking risks that most climbers would not even contemplate, recognizes fear as a warning sign to stop: "Fear tightens you up too much. If I start to feel weird, I'll back off a route." Listening to one's body can mean the difference between life and death in sports like solo climbing. When the risks are not so high, self-awareness—and acting on that self-awareness—can prevent injury. Athletes are often driven to push beyond pain and keep going when their bodies are screaming out for them to stop or slow down. To achieve maximum potential an athlete does need to go beyond his comfort zone. However, there are times when the signals the body gives are warning of injury, and the smart athlete listens and responds to his body.

FEEDBACK IN FLOW

When athletes are in flow, the feedback appears clear and precise, and it assists in keeping the mind focused. There is no need to stop and reflect on how well things are going. There is a feeling of certainty, of everything falling into place. The feedback tells the athlete that she is progressing toward her goals. To describe how this feels, athletes refer to everything going like clockwork, being in harmony, feeling like it clicks. Here is how another figure skater describes the feedback she receives about her performance in flow:

You can really feel what is going on. . . . One of the things is that you are really aware of your body within this flow state. Ah, you know everything, you can feel every finger and every toe and everything, so you know exactly what your body is doing—which is why everything works so well.

Learning to use feedback to further develop one's skills and to enhance progress toward one's goals is important for reasons that go beyond skill development. It may mean that when everything does come together in performance, flow can be maintained by skillful use of feedback. What one does becomes worth doing for its own sake, regardless of winning or losing.

Of course winning a race, getting a medal and one's picture in the papers, gives a warm feeling and a boost to the morale. But working for external recognition only leaves you at the mercy of fickle fate—there are so many things beyond your control that can decide the outcome. A competitor in better shape or a slight difference in conditions might snatch the prize from your grasp and leave you disappointed. If you enjoy the performance for its own sake, experiencing involvement each moment of the way, then doing sport is worth the energy expended regardless of what happens in the end.

chapter

7

Focusing on the Present

Doing well in sport, whether at the amateur or the most elite levels of performance, requires undivided attention. If the mind starts wandering, the body starts getting out of sync. And it is not only performance that suffers then, but the quality of experience as well. We cannot enjoy what we don't notice. Every second that the mind is distracted from the sport activity is lost—we don't experience it, we cannot savor it or recall it.

Undivided attention is hard to come by. In everyday life we are usually distracted by external events or the mind's ruminations. It is hard to concentrate when there are dozens of tasks to attend to or when we keep thinking about wrongs we suffered in the past. One of the great things about sport is that it makes it possible to forget the problems of everyday life, and concentrate exclusively on a doable, exciting activity. As a teenager from an inner city says about what happens when he starts playing basketball:

Sometimes on court I think of a problem, like fighting with my steady girl, and I think that's nothing compared to the game. You can think about a problem all day but as soon as you get in the game, the hell with it!

But even in sport it is not always easy to keep the mind from wandering. To know how to focus and be able to maintain concentration throughout an event is a mental challenge for athletes at all levels.

And not just for athletes—coaches also face the challenge of maintaining focus on the important issues, not getting sidetracked, in order to keep their athletes thinking appropriately. Spectators also need to be able to keep their focus on the sport event in front of them if they are going to experience and enjoy it fully.

THE PRESENT—A ROAD TO FLOW

So what is the right focus? This of course depends on what is most effective for the situation in question. There is no one right or wrong way to concentrate. However, there is an important principle: flow depends on a present-centered focus, where the person is totally connected with the activity. Concentration on the task at hand is the most obvious feature of being in flow.

Unfortunately this is not the simple task it appears to be on the surface. Our minds are not easily programmed to stay in the moment. The ability to take in large amounts of information cognitively can make it difficult to sustain attention on any one thing for a period of time. Thoughts about the past or the future often clamor for attention when we engage in an activity. Yet learning to stay in the present is an essential skill for athletes and coaches wanting to experience flow. Understanding why it can be so difficult is the first step to controlling thought processes.

The Past—A Road to Nowhere

Athletes and coaches often fall prey to two *what ifs:* What might have been and what should have happened. The shot that *almost* went in, the play that *should have been* made, or the time that was run *last year* are not helpful thoughts when individuals are performing, but they are examples of where athletes' minds go when the going gets tough.

It is true that in order to benefit from feedback one must correct performance as it takes place, and that means paying attention to why the last shot was missed or the last lap was run too slowly. Tactical adjustments require noticing the results of one's past actions. But to be effective, concentration on what just happened should be quick and clinical. Ideally, monitoring one's performance should become so automatic that one does not need to think about it. During a peak performance athletes notice, evaluate, and fine-tune performance without even being conscious that they are doing so. And if they let emotions interfere with evaluation, the game is as good as lost. Focusing on what happened or what could or should have been will not change the past, nor will it help the present. It is taking a road that leads nowhere. The past cannot be brought back, but the present can suffer as a consequence of trying.

The Future—A Road Under Construction

Just as the past is not the place for an athlete's mind to be, neither is the future. Thinking ahead prevents paying full attention to the present and stands in the way of experiencing it fully. The future cannot be controlled; it is an emerging presence that unfolds as we remain centered in the present. The future is a road under construction. Eventually it will be the road we want to be on, but not while it is still in the making.

A swimmer recounts a race where her thoughts raced ahead to the finish and the effect it had on her performance:

> Soon as I got in the pool, I thought, "Right, this is it." As soon as I got in the water, my stroke was flowing and I felt great. And down the first 50—as soon as that—I went, "Oh my God, I'm winning, I'm going to win!" And as soon as I thought that is when everything fell apart, and I just lost it.

Winning is a strong motivation for many athletes, and wanting to win can be inspiring, especially when we feel it is within our grasp. But the danger of focusing ahead to the outcome we anticipate is, as this swimmer said, that we can easily lose what it is we are striving for. Taking focus away from what you are doing is a sure way to break the flow.

Getting Back on the Right Road

A present-centered focus is one in which all the concentration is directed to what is happening in the present moment. That is, your focus is on the ball that is coming toward you, the stroke that you are making, the feeling of the maneuver you are performing. This is where flow happens—in the present moment. The challenge rises, however, when the length of the time you need to stay focused on the present extends beyond what you are accustomed to.

Unfortunately, what most athletes are used to is not a very long period of time; most sport events last longer than we are trained to keep our attention focused. However, when a player really enjoys the experience, it is possible to sustain unbroken attention for long periods of time, as this football player describes:

> All I remember in that game is that I never noticed anything for the whole 80 minutes of the game, so never at any time in the game was

my concentration broken. The other thing—in games sometimes you hesitate and think a bit—that was a game where everything seemed to just happen, rather than [my] consciously thinking about what was happening.

Staying totally focused on the present moment can give the impression that things happen effortlessly, as they did for this player. That is because the plans and evaluations that usually occupy the mind as we perform are not part of the picture; all that we are aware of is the present moment.

To get a good idea of how long you can keep your thoughts focused on the present try this simple meditation exercise.

Meditation Exercise

Sit in a comfortable position where you will not be disturbed. Take a note of the time on your watch. Close your eyes and focus on one thing (for instance, your breathing). Pay attention to your breaths in and out. Do this for as long as you maintain only this focus. Open your eyes when your focus moves and note the time on your watch. How much time passed since you began this exercise? One minute? Twenty seconds? Perhaps you were able to maintain a focus on your breathing for five minutes?

Most people who do this exercise without having trained in meditation or thought control find it difficult to maintain a singular focus on their breathing for long. Thoughts pop into their heads, and no sooner has one stray thought been extinguished than another enters the consciousness, demanding attention. This scattered thinking is what the Zen monks call the "monkey-mind." If this is the case when you are sitting with your eyes closed and no distractions present, what is likely to happen when you are performing a sport with all the environmental, social, and physical stimuli that are part of the activity? Most likely your attention will be caught by several different factors, none of which is directly relevant to the task at hand. It is only when all mental energies are directed toward the task at hand, however, that the absorbing state of flow can occur. What do you do when you find distracting thoughts disrupting your focus? The skill of refocusing allows a person to return to the right focus, and that is what we turn to next.

KEYS TO STAYING FOCUSED IN THE PRESENT

It is a highly disciplined athlete who can keep the focus tuned into her performance for the duration of an event, particularly when that event lasts longer than a 100-meter sprint. Although the goal is to stay focused without any lapses in concentration, most athletes find this a difficult task.

Refocus

Refocusing is a skill that can allow athletes to regain lost focus. It is like tuning back into the right mental channel when distracting thoughts occur. The first step in refocusing is to become aware of the slip in attention. The sooner this can occur, the less will be the disruption to performance. Once an inappropriate focus has been recognized, you want to be rid of it.

To facilitate this, the second step is choosing another focal point or direction of attention that the mind can turn to. Often this will be the same focus of attention as before the concentration was disrupted. But in a constantly moving and changing sport environment, the right focus depends on what is happening at each moment in time. Thus, concentration becomes fluid, not static. Knowing what to focus on is a skill that athletes and coaches develop over time and through exposure to different scenarios. By learning to store these scenarios and responses in memory, you can enhance the ability to respond swiftly, in a short space of time. This maximizes the effectiveness of your response; moreover, it helps you achieve or return to flow during performance.

Use Task Goals

Whether you direct focus toward the past, present, or future has an important bearing on whether the flow state occurs. So too does *what* you focus on. The distinction between outcome and task *goals* has already been discussed in chapter 5, where we emphasized the advantages of task goals over outcome goals. The type of *focus* you take into an athletic event can also be described in terms of task or outcome characteristics.

A task focus describes concentrating on the specific challenges of the event. It may include technique or strategy points, executing plays, or simply being involved in the game. A task focus keeps the attention directed toward what needs to be accomplished in the moment.

An outcome focus, on the other hand, is concerned with outperforming others; the focus is on how one is doing in relation to other performers. Almost every athlete will find himself making some comparisons with his competitors at some point, and this is not necessarily a bad thing. But if an individual's focus stays on the competitors and comparative evaluations, attention is taken away from where it needs to be, which is on the actual performance. Thinking about what others are doing and constantly comparing oneself to competitors takes away psychic energy from the tasks to be performed. It also takes the focus out of the present moment. The potential for flow thus decreases as the outcome focus increases.

Keep it Simple

Being in flow is not a mindless trance in which you are simply carried along by the activity, oblivious to all that is taking place. The Southern Californian mantra "Go with the flow" refers to almost the opposite type of flow from what we are talking about: it implies a laissez-faire attitude, where one is taken along as if on a ride that requires no effort of one's own. Flow requires deep concentration—but you do not arrive at it by trying to concentrate with all your might or by trying to fill the mind with as many thoughts as you can.

Yes, you can think too much. Thinking too hard or too much implies strain and overanalysis. Flow is about being relaxed with what you are doing and how you are thinking. Filling your mind with many thoughts while you are performing will keep you from being fully immersed in what it is you are doing. The old adage about keeping it simple is a good strategy for overanalytical thinkers. A hockey player describes how keeping things simple allowed her mind to relax:

> I like to keep it really simple. I always like to take what might be [called] 20 points down to 3 or 4 points and keep everything simple and clear. Then your mind can relax.

How many ideas or strategy points an athlete wants to focus on during performance is very much an individual choice, one that will also vary according to the particular sport's demands. The principle to keep in mind is not to become overly analytic in your desire to take an active cognitive approach to performance.

Plan for the Competition

Having just argued against thinking too much, we are going to recommend a strategy that involves considerable thought about one's performance. The secret is to choose carefully *when* this thinking takes place. A competition plan is prepared well in advance of the event, and it involves working out where to focus at different parts of an event. By preparing mental plans in advance, the athlete is freed to carry out the plan during performance.

The more a competition plan is rehearsed ahead of time, in training and simulated competitive situations, the more automatic it will become. As a result, less analysis and planning will be required during the actual performance. Sports vary in how easily they accommodate specific mental plans that are worked out in advance of the event. Some, like running and swimming, are well-suited to detailed plans: the event can be broken into smaller segments, and specific goals and focus points can be developed for each segment. Other sports that are more interactive, including ball games and most team sports, involve unfolding strategies and plays that cannot be totally prepared in advance. In these types of sports, plans for set plays and critical situations that are well-rehearsed and understood by all players can facilitate total involvement and the right focus.

Every sport will vary in its structure, and so, too, will the format of a mental plan. By using the structure of your sport, you can devise your own plan for how to achieve optimal concentration during your event.

One of the main advantages of mental plans is that they help keep an athlete's mind on the task. It is easy to lose concentration or to never get really focused if you haven't thought ahead of time about what you want to accomplish at various points in the performance. Even so, it takes discipline to follow the plan when it really counts— when the pressure is on during competition. A runner describes how he would lose focus by moving away from his plan:

> Being distracted, losing concentration, losing your focus on where you are at that point; going more to the outcome as opposed to the segment of your plan—losing focus on the plan.

Make Backup Plans

Even the best-laid plans can falter or fall apart in the heat of the moment. This is when a backup plan comes into play. Backup plans are developed by preparing responses, or refocusing strategies, to use in adverse competitive situations. You can plan for a potential repeat of situations that you may have experienced in the past and for new potential problems whose occurrence might have a deleterious effect on performance. Of course, it is not possible to plan for all possible

distracting or difficult scenarios, and to do so would take a lot of the fun and spontaneity out of the sport. But working out in advance how you would respond in potentially event-decisive situations can facilitate an appropriate response being made when the heat is on. Knowing you have a backup strategy should something unexpected arise will boost your self-confidence and allow you to focus on the task at hand.

Practice Concentration

Mental plans are only as effective as an athlete's ability to concentrate effectively. It is not much use having a detailed plan if the athlete can't keep his attention on its various components. Concentration is an all-important skill, and many a coach has been heard admonishing players from the sideline, "Concentrate!" In an interview an athlete summed up why this dimension of focus is so important: "Concentration totally engrosses you in the game, so I guess to achieve flow state you need to have good powers of concentration."

Being able to maintain an appropriate focus is the skill that will determine how effectively any plan can be carried out. How to achieve these powers of concentration is the topic of many books and countless self-help courses. It is a skill developed through practice, like all mental skills.

Knowing what to concentrate on is the first step, and this is where plans play an important role. A basic principle for developing concentration abilities is to practice focusing in ways that simulate the types of concentration particularly needed for your sport.

If a narrow intent focus is required, as in a gymnastics routine, you can practice that type of focus in exercises that last a time period similar to that of the actual competitive routine; this practice helps you develop the concentration skills needed for the specific event. If your sport involves taking in large amounts of information from lots of different directions, as a soccer game does, practicing to maintain focus in situations where you must take in information from a diverse number of sources will be helpful.

Developing your own concentration activities and routines that suit both the demands of the sport and your own style is likely to be most effective. As an illustration of how a concentration routine might proceed, an elite figure skater describes the routine he follows before every competition to achieve his best focus:

> OK, the first thing I do as I get close to the competition, within the hour: I focus on the ice and I look at the ice rink. No one is in the arena yet, and I just look at it and say, it's mine, that's my time. And

then I take it from the ice to . . . there's the ice, there's myself, and there's my partner. There's nothing else, nothing else matters. Nothing else matters. And I tell myself that, and I make myself believe that. And then anything that interferes with that has to be turned into a positive—or disregarded. And I stay there for an hour. And that's not easy to do.

This skater has found a concentration routine that brings him to a point of readiness: his focus is totally engulfed by the ice, himself, and his partner. Each athlete needs to find what the best focus for himself is and then follow a routine that will lead to finding that focus in competition.

As one becomes experienced, it is possible to achieve concentration just by putting on one's athletic shoes or by walking into the stadium. Basketball superstar Michael Jordan developed a superior ability to focus on the present. He says, "Each time I step on the basketball court, I never know what will happen. I live for the moment. I play for the moment."

Direct Your Attention

Where athletes direct attention varies according to the demands of the sport, and that focus will change as the task demands vary. However, even in sports that on the surface would seem to rely on certain types of attentional focus, athletes vary in what they find works best. In rowing, for example, you might suppose a narrow focus would be most appropriate, and often rowers describe staying "within their own boat" when they are in flow. However, for other rowers, directing at least some attention to what is going on around them works well. Here is one rower's approach:

I can look at what somebody else is doing, yet rely totally on the feeling senses of the body. The nerve endings in the body are so in tune with the environment and the dynamics of the sport that you can let your mind, your eyes at least, picture . . . things outside. . . . That's having fun competing in your sport.

For this athlete, looking around was part of what made him able to stay completely focused on the rhythms of his body—and what made the activity more fun. But looking around at what is happening outside your own performance is generally not recommended because of the likelihood of becoming distracted and drawn into thinking about what others are doing. Of course, in some sports performance is dictated by what others are doing, and it is critical to be aware of the big picture around you. Most team sports require the ability to take in or see the field of play, so as to anticipate the moves of the other players on both teams.

Beyond the actual performance area, however, is another environment, which can be either a distraction or a source of motivation: the crowd. Competing in front of large crowds can be stressful, especially when the other team or an athlete other than yourself is the crowd's favorite. Some athletes focus on blocking out the crowd, while others actually enjoy taking in the atmosphere. Again, there is no right or wrong way to focus, but instead it is a matter of finding what works best for you, what will help you to find the right CS balance in a particular situation. A football player describes how he dealt with playing in front of large crowds:

> On some occasions in games, a crowd of 60,000 plus can be scattering to your mind and may induce concern. But playing in big games you find, for the most part, you shut it out. You're there aware of the aura and the noise and the singing, but then you come to a microworld down there, where there is only yourselves.

The important thing, as this athlete reports, is to dissociate the emotional content from the noise and the "aura" of the crowd. Many people can't entirely tune out the sensory distraction, but as long as they don't let it affect their feelings, the distraction need not detract from concentration.

Concentration in sport is not necessarily a solitary experience. Other people—competitors as well as teammates—can also help us achieve focus, instead of their being a source of distraction. A pairs rower, in describing the focus of flow, put it this way: "Nothing else gets into your head." For her, when both she and her rowing partner experienced this total focus, it was (in her words) "an awesome experience." Knowing your partner or teammates are simultaneously experiencing the same optimal state you are in can heighten the intensity that flow provides. This being so in tune with teammates as well as the performance is what makes team sports so fulfilling for many athletes.

Experiencing flow does, of course, become a greater challenge when interaction between teammates is part of the event; not only does one athlete have to get her focus right, so too do the other team members. Another rower, who competed in an eight, described the difficulty of keeping focused in his event:

© Claus Andersen

If it's going well, it's easy to get into the flow . . . but if it's not, then you can't. So it all comes back to the team—everybody, all the guys, knitted in together. And it just rolls along for 5 or 10 minutes, half an hour, going very well, but then someone might lose concentration or go off beat or something. And then you'd be out of that situation; you can't have any control over that.

Interestingly, this rower thought that if he were in a single sculls event, staying in flow would be much more controllable. The bonus of team flow apparently comes at the price of giving up some personal autonomy and control.

Finding what attentional focus helps to bring about complete mental involvement in your performance is the key principle for finding flow. It may mean concentrating in a unique way or, on the other hand, following what is generally recommended in a particular situation for that sport. Practicing with different ways of directing the attention is useful for gaining flexibility in your attentional skills and also for finding your keys to becoming totally absorbed in performing.

TOTAL IMMERSION IN THE PRESENT

When all of the conditions for flow are present—clear goals, a steady stream of feedback, a matching of challenges and skills—concentration becomes more intense. Yet, paradoxically, it also seems more spontaneous. In other words, while the attention is sharp and focused, it needs no effort to keep it so. When reading a boring textbook, in contrast, you might find yourself having to constantly force the mind to focus on the page and decode the words as you go along. You struggle to keep other ideas from entering your mind. But when you read an exciting novel, your eyes probably race through the pages effortlessly and you forget everything else beyond the plot of the story. Similarly when sport is going well, the demands of the activity easily absorb all the attention.

A figure skater does a good job of trying to describe the apparent paradox of effortless effort that is so typical of focus in flow:

> Well, it is a total focus, but it's a balance really, between a total focus and a total release in a way. Because you are totally focused . . . . On the other hand, it is also happening on its own. It is like it is a total automatic process. It's kind of like the focus is even an automatic thing. The things you are saying to yourself throughout the whole performance are automatic in a way. They're the things that you've said to yourself over and over and over again in training. It is like you are taking all of the good parts of all of your training, and they are happening automatically.

In a flow state, concentration is much easier to sustain than in non-flow experiences. Describing the ease of concentration that occurs in flow, the skater says it happens as if automatically. The fact that concentration happens more effortlessly in flow is one of the reasons it is such an enjoyable state to be in. Staying focused on what you are doing ceases to be a struggle or a strain, and this allows complete involvement, which is a very satisfying state to experience.

When an experience is so intense that it requires literally all our attention to process its details, there might not be enough psychic energy left over to transfer the experience into memory. So while we know that something awesome has happened, we might not be able to recall what exactly it was. Here is how one skater describes such an intense flow experience:

I remember another performance like that, but I don't really remember anything specific about it. We got off the ice, and I couldn't tell you one thing: it was a blank, like "What just happened out there?" And another time I remember a lot of very specific things. . . . I just remember how the ice felt and . . . every little detail. And another time it just floated by, and I couldn't tell you a thing about it really.

Others also mention a floating sensation and lack of memory afterward for the details. Here is a rower describing a similar occurrence:

It was funny, it was like at the end of it you couldn't remember what had happened. It was like a strange trance the whole time, and it was like just really knowing what you were going to do. And it's like you've done it all before so it's easy; you know, just no one else can interfere or get in the way of anything. Like [being] mesmerized by it.

When the experience is so intense that it requires every bit of attention, the person can no longer process information even about his or her existence. She loses her sense of identity, like an automaton proceeding in a trance. In such moments flow resembles those states of ecstasy that religious disciplines reach through ritual, prayer, or meditation. For instance, the floating sensation described by athletes is reminiscent of the concept of *yu*, which the Chinese Taoists prescribed as the "right way to live." *Yu* has been translated to mean "floating," "flowing," or "walking without touching the ground." At such levels of intensity concentration is not only effortless, but it also achieves a pure, spiritual dimension beyond the body whose efforts made it possible in the first place.

We enjoy sport for a variety of reasons such as the physical well-being it helps produce, the exhilaration of victory, and the ability to forget the hassles of everyday life. But perhaps the most satisfying reward sport can give is this full immersion in *the now*, the effortless stretching of mind and body in a totally experienced present.

8

Controlling the Controllables

We rarely feel that what we do in everyday life is entirely under our control. There are always so many unpredictable events that affect people: the company someone works for could decide to downsize and an individual loses her job; a virus might get in the bloodstream and a person gets ill; a man's partner could decide that she no longer likes him and he is left alone. At every moment, we are vulnerable to dozens of potentially threatening forces hovering just beyond the boundaries of awareness.

One of the most satisfying aspects of sport is that it offers a temporary shelter from the chaos of everyday life. While involved in sport, we can forget the looming threats and focus entirely on an activity that is potentially under our control. The rules of most games are clear; they limit what can happen and exclude everything else. If we are well prepared, chances are we can cope with anything that comes our way.

A dancer describes the reassuring feeling she gets at such moments of involvement:

A strong relaxation and calmness comes over me. I have no worries of failure. What a powerful and warm feeling it is! I want to expand, hug the world. I feel enormous power to effect something of grace and beauty.

Of course, we are never entirely in control, even in the most intense flow experience. Flow occurs at the point of balance between skills

and challenges: the possibility of challenges suddenly increasing and tipping us out of flow is always present. What is important, however, is the knowledge that in principle we have the *possibility* of keeping things under control. If we are well prepared and keep focused, we can stay master of the performance. In the words of a young basketball player:

> I feel in control. Sure. I've practiced and have a good feeling for the shots I can make. . . . I don't feel in control of the other player— even if he's bad and I know where to beat him. It's me and not him that I'm working on.

Ultimately, control in sport is not about opponents or external obstacles. It is about learning to discipline a wandering mind, fluttering emotions, an unsteady will. Sport creates the possibility of achieving control over the self.

ROLE OF CONTROL IN FLOW

Feeling in control conveys a sense of security and power that people in all walks of life seek. Some spend their lives accumulating more and more money or power so they can achieve control over their environments. The attraction of control rests at least partly with the dread of its opposite. Feeling out of control can be a scary experience and carries with it worry and other negative emotions. Being unable to influence what is happening to you and around you creates feelings of helplessness and inadequacy. These feelings break down confidence and make us pull back from involvement and risk.

> Among the many wise suggestions that legendary UCLA basketball coach John Wooden made was "Do not let what you cannot do interfere with what you can do."

Moving From Comfort to Flow

To stay in flow one must keep extending challenges and skills, as well as maintaining them in balance; this growth is at odds with feeling control. Lack of confidence may keep you from taking the risks associated with challenging situations. Putting yourself in situations where there are great challenges means also opening up to the possibility of feeling out of control and not succeeding. This may lead to choices of staying at a certain level of achievement or putting out effort only in situations where there is a good chance of success.

Though such strategies will ensure comfortable feelings, they will not lead to growth. It is not possible to improve without running risks. Winning a major championship is a tremendous accomplishment. However, to win the next one or to move one's skills upward requires stepping out of the comfort zone and stepping into the flow zone. This is a zone defined by the delicate balance of challenges and skills, with both being extended to personal limits.

Athletes who describe being in flow often mention having strong feelings of control. Take this runner, for example, describing a race in which she experienced flow:

> I ran a personal best. I felt very in control. I felt very strong. I was able to run as I had planned without too much trouble. I felt really focused. I just felt like, you know, like . . . it clicked.

She then elaborated on how it felt to her to be in control:

> It is being totally in control of what's going through your head, and totally in control of your own body and how hard you're pushing, and to be able to go faster when you say, "OK, let's put on a bit of a sprint or let's drop this person." And being able to do it and being in total control of what's going through your head. Like if pain comes to you, to be able to say, "OK, fine, I expected this. That's all right. I'm not going to dwell on it." And to be able to do that . . . get away from it . . . total mental and physical control.

Although these are obviously very real perceptions, staying in flow means that one is at the cutting edge of performance, where challenges and skills are fluid and apt to change. It is sort of like moving your center of gravity to the edge to improve your performance. If one were really in total control and stayed in this state, skills would become greater than challenges, and the intensity of flow would yield to a feeling of relaxation and eventually to boredom.

It is for this reason that the feeling of total control, like the feeling of flow, is so fleeting: by the nature of things it is impossible to experience either of them for any length of time. As soon as we become comfortable with a certain level of control, we are in danger of losing flow. At that point, it's time to move on to higher challenges, to move into new areas of risk and uncertainty. If we are lucky, we will again reach a moment of control at a higher level of skills, and experience flow at a new point of equilibrium, and so on, in a constantly extending spiral of increasing complexity of performance.

Riding the Razor

Often it is the skills side of the equation that is under threat among athletes. Confidence is unstable and at the mercy of competitive outcomes. Challenges are ever present, especially at the upper ends of athletic competition. This may be why athletes report feelings of control, especially in connection with some of their most memorable performances, when the experience stands out from average sport encounters. A figure skater describes it as "riding on the razor":

> Riding on the razor . . . it's like practice, you can sharpen it, make the razor thinner; but you can fall one way or the other, and I think that's like the stressors can tip it. But once you're in that groove, it just seems like nothing can go wrong.

During these golden moments, athletes are not faced with uncertainty about what they are going to do or concern that they may not have the necessary skills. Losing these shackles is empowering, and it is why, once experienced, flow becomes a much sought-after state.

KEYS TO BALANCING CONTROL AND RELEASE

The feeling of control in flow generally occurs below the surface of awareness. If we spent energy focusing on trying to be in control, we would not have sufficient resources to fully invest ourselves in the activity. When we can get to the point of no longer worrying about control, we are getting closer to flow. For this attitude indicates absorption in the task and confidence that being out of control will not be an issue. Therefore, releasing the desire to be in control can paradoxically result in more control. Once we have put in place the preparation and necessary controllable factors, forgetting about controlling and instead being fully involved in the activity holds the key to flow.

Find the Optimal Control Level

We can all recall instances when we've felt out of control, or out of our depth, in sport. The feelings are intense and lead to calling into question our skills and reasons for being there. Losing can do it, especially if the margin is wide and there is little opportunity to demonstrate any skill. Embarrassing oneself with low skills or poor decisions can create uncomfortable, negative feelings, and sport, by its

public nature, accentuates feelings of being evaluated by others. Wanting to do well, and not being able to do so, can lead to skyrocketing anxiety.

All of these situations lead to feelings of being out of control and take away the potential for enjoyment. In terms of the flow model described in chapter 3, when the challenges are far greater than the skills, we have little chance of feeling in control and instead feel anxious. Regaining control is necessary to bring confidence levels back up to the perceived challenges, to restore the CS balance. This can be achieved by either redefining the challenge in terms that can be attained or by increasing confidence levels to the point where the challenge is reachable.

Can there be too much control in sport? Surely the more control, the better? Not according to the flow model: when the scales balance in favor of skills over challenges, that can decrease the quality of experience, just as surely as can having challenges that are too high.

Knowing for certain you are going to be successful takes away motivation and focus. What is the point of trying to do your best when the outcome is a foregone conclusion? Sport rarely offers certain outcomes; because of this, too much control is generally less of an issue in sport than experiencing a lack of control. But it is important to recognize that part of the attraction of dedicating yourself to the pursuit of a goal is that the outcome is not a certainty. When the goal is achieved, through application and belief in yourself, the experience is much more satisfying than when you work toward a foregone conclusion.

Recognize the Controllables

There are certain factors in the sport environment that are controllable and others that are beyond our reach. Our own performance is within our control, for example, as are our responses to what happens to and around us. What our competitors or the officials do is not within our control. Recognizing the difference between aspects we can control and those we cannot allows us to be well-prepared and well aware of the challenges we face. Without preparation and paying attention to certain aspects of performance, you place your skills at risk of being insufficient for the upcoming challenges. Therefore, it is important to set the stage for flow through preparation. A dedicated athlete might write down a list of the most crucial elements before each event, and then check off those items that are already under control and note those where further preparation is needed. Table 8.1 is an example of a control checklist for competition. In the first column,

Table 8.1

Control Checklist for Competition

Factors for optimal performance	Under control? Yes or No	Further preparation needed
Long-term factors (e.g., rest, diet, practice)		
Short-term factors (e.g., competition goals, visualizing event, looking forward to having a great time)		

note the important factors (long and short term) that lead to optimal performance in your sport. In the second column, indicate whether you have each of these factors under control. For each factor not currently under control, use the third column to specify the further preparation needed to bring the factor more within your control.

Set the Stage

What aspects of performance should you take into account when preparing for an important event? In most sports there are a myriad of preparatory areas that need attention. Physical fitness, appropriate diet, physical readiness, mental skills, technical factors, equipment, course familiarity, travel—the list is long, and within each of these areas, of course, are many sub-areas. The extent to which you can optimally prepare each relevant factor affects the resultant experience. Preparing thoroughly means that the controllables have been attended to.

Simon, our cyclist, illustrates how an athlete in his preparation sets the stage for a successful and memorable flow experience while racing:

> My form was up, and everything physically was on: flexibility was up, strength was up, climbing abilities were up, recovery was up. Everything was spot on. My style was spot on, even my eating was right. Circumstances just allowed it to be the best possible chance to do it. And so I felt the only things I'll have to fight against are inevitable mishaps, like punctures and things—and they happened, but I had the mental energy to get around them.

In this example, Simon describes how his taking care of the important controllables in his sport set the stage for what turned into an optimal cycling experience. By paying close attention to preparation ahead of time, there is more mental energy available to cope with the challenges—some of which may not be controllable—as they occur during performance.

Recognize the Feel of Optimal Energy

Sport psychology contends that there are ways to explain and predict the optimal amounts of arousal or anxiety for competitive performance. For each person there is an optimal level of anxiety that will facilitate good performance. Experienced athletes who are in tune with their bodies recognize when their energy levels are not optimal. Sometimes the problem is lacking energy, resulting in feeling sluggish and having delayed responses. More often in competition the problem is having uncontrolled energy, which is experienced as nervousness or worry. So, while feeling too relaxed can be a problem at times, not being relaxed enough is a more common symptom of non-optimal energy levels.

The first step to gaining control of energy levels is being able to recognize what an optimal energy zone feels like. Each athlete will have her own optimal level and with this level will be associated certain feelings that the athlete comes to recognize as indicating readiness. An elite skater describes it this way:

> There's a certain frame of mind where you're calm, but you're nervous; I mean your stomach doesn't feel right, and you know you're

nervous, but you're not going around screaming like you're out of control; you can sort of control your energy and control your nervousness and try and turn it into energy for you.

It is important to know what you are trying to attain in controlling energy levels. The kind of energy needed for a basketball game is clearly different than that required for a game of chess. Even within one sport individuals will vary widely in what is optimal for themselves. Working out what is right is a process of reflecting on past performances and energy levels associated with them, experimenting with different combinations, and developing skills in being able to modify existing levels.

Knowing Your Optimal Energy Level

Think about times when you have been both happy with your performance and with your energy levels during it. Try to describe what it feels like when you are in your optimal energy zone. Having a good picture of what you are trying to attain is the first step to getting there again!

Relaxation techniques can be used to gain control over energy and assist in the development of other mental skills. For example, concentration skills are affected by arousal levels, with a moderate amount of arousal facilitating focus but too little or too much making it difficult to concentrate effectively.

Just like the relationship of control to flow, the relationship of energy levels to optimal experience is a fine balancing act. A swimmer explains why it is difficult to stay on the diagonal that represents the optimal balance between challenges and skills:

> I've got to be relaxed, but I've also got to be hyped up; it's almost in between—sort of anxious and sort of relaxed. It's a fine line, because if I'm too relaxed, I'm just downhill, and if I'm too anxious, I'm downhill, too.

Choose Your Responses to Competition

What happens in competition is sometimes controllable, sometimes not. How you *choose* to react to what happens is entirely within your control, and this provides an enormous source of power. Unfortunately, this power is often an untapped resource because athletes either do not recognize that they are free to choose how to respond or because they have learned ineffective reactions.

Sometimes an opponent is simply superior. You have no control over that unless you're in charge of scheduling the competition. Although you may influence the level of another's performance, rarely can you orchestrate it. As skiing great A.J. Kitt said, "You have no control over what the other guy does. You only have control over what you do."

When an umpire's decision goes against you, or the opposition does something outside of the rules or spirit of the game, or you make a judgment error, you can choose to become upset and distracted or to let go of the unwanted occurrence and move on with the game. There will always be decisions made that you are certain are unfair or biased, subtle and not-so-subtle breaking of rules, and situations that cannot be predicted or controlled. These have potential for serious disruption—or they can serve as reminders to focus on the controllable aspects of your performance. In the heat of the moment it can be difficult to choose the more objective and resourceful response, and this is why preparing your refocusing strategies (see chapter 7) is important. It is much easier to choose effective responses when egos and emotions are not in the way. Learning to respond effectively in frustrating or difficult situations increases control, and while the situations themselves may not always be controllable, the responses always are.

Pat Riley, one of the NBA's all-time "winningest" coaches, proffers this approach amid adversity: "When you're playing against a stacked deck, compete even harder. Show the world how much you'll fight for the winner's circle. If you do, someday the cellophane will crackle off a fresh pack, one that belongs to you, and the cards will be stacked in your favor."

A rower who believed flow was controllable argued strongly that achieving this state was up to the individual:

If it's not going well, change it, do something that makes it go well. And the only person responsible for getting yourself into that flow state is you. You're responsible for your own environment, so that's the key to it, you know, making yourself responsible for yourself. And you know when you're into it, and hold it there, and produce more.

We will address the issue of the control of flow later in this chapter, as well as in the epilogue. The key point here is that you are in control of how you respond to what happens to you, that is, you are responsible for your own thoughts and actions.

Staying Cool When the Heat Is On

Recognizing that you are in control of how you respond is easy enough at a theoretical level, but the real test comes when the pressure is on. A world champion triathlete, in discussing her perceptions of whether flow was controllable, thought that if all the factors were there, she would have control, but that as the event neared, it could be difficult to keep it. She illustrated with this story:

> A good example for me was in the World Champs. . . . It was ridiculous, but someone was meant to deliver me a new wheel that I was riding in the race. And now I can tell anybody [to] never, never worry about it, never get a new wheel before a race. It's no big deal anyway. Well, I just totally flipped because our bikes had to be in by six o'clock that night—and by six o'clock my wheel hadn't arrived and I just absolutely flipped out. . . . I just completely blew my race. I had one of the worst races I've ever had—I got fourth, and to some degree that should have been within my control, just to be able to sit down and say, it doesn't matter about a stupid wheel. But because of all the factors that make a person an elite athlete, it was sort of a little bit out of my control. I felt it was out of my control, because all someone had to do was deliver me a wheel, and I would never let anybody else down that way, especially a person who's the reigning world champion. But all of a sudden, I wasn't in control at all. I should have been in a perfect flow state; I'd been racing fabulous up to it. I had a great race the week before: I'd beaten everybody by a long way and my confidence was up. But, as I said, about 13 or 14 hours before my race everything got blown out, so I didn't get any flow state at all."

As the triathlete's story illustrates, as the time to compete draws near, staying in control of your responses becomes increasingly difficult. It is especially difficult if you believe that the performance will depend on an external support—in the triathlete's case, the new wheel for her bike. To the extent that you imagine that success will depend on something external, you give up control and become vulnerable to a failure you cannot do anything about. It is critical to keep the reins of performance firmly in hand before and during competition to ensure that the weeks, months, or even years of preparation will come together for an optimal experience.

FEELING INVINCIBLE

Exercising control in difficult situations is very satisfying. It leads to feeling powerful and a sense of being able to make a difference. Stepping out of the secure position of guaranteed success into the unknown and uncertain field of high challenge, where there is some doubt as to what the outcome will be, and then *exercising control* enhances the self immeasurably. This is where the enjoyment from the control aspect of flow comes from—not from exerting control when nothing or very little is at stake, but doing so when the challenges are extending beyond your present reach.

Meeting high challenges with unwavering confidence allows previously unimaginable events to occur. Here a rugby player, matched against a superior opponent, describes an experience he had during a game:

> You can't imagine anything going wrong. Like my opposite number was a very good player, probably one of the two best wingers in the world. At the start of the game I could imagine myself missing him in tackles, whereas at the end of the game there was no way that he was ever going to beat me. Even though he's probably a far better player, I couldn't even consider that at the end of the game.

Athletes who are continually seeking to extend their limits and who have the necessary commitment to keep developing their skills to keep pace with the ever-increasing challenges experience a tremendous sense of accomplishment from continuing to move their achievements to higher levels. Such athletes also experience the exhilaration of flow in what they are doing, as did Simon, who describes feeling invincible during this state:

> Your mind doesn't wander from the job, your body feels great, everything runs; nothing, just nothing can go wrong. And you believe that nothing will go wrong, and there's nothing that will be able to stop you or stand in your way. And you're ready to tackle anything, and you don't fear any possibility happening. And the possibilities do happen, you tackle them, and they go by, and nothing leaves its mark on you. And you go on to the next task, and it's just exhilarating.

The energy Simon experienced cycling in this instance is obvious. A hockey player describes another aspect of feeling invincible—a tremendous sense of calm:

> I just had a feeling of absolute calm. Like everything's going right for you, that whatever you're going to do, even your teammates, you knew that they were going to do it right.

SEEKING TO CONTROL FLOW ITSELF

People wishing to be able to call upon flow experiences more often sometimes ask whether this special state can be controlled. It is not possible to make flow happen at will (an issue addressed in the epilogue), and attempting to do so will only make the state more elusive. However, removing obstacles and providing facilitating conditions will increase its occurrence—and how to set the stage for flow is what this book is about.

Athletes vary widely in their responses when they're asked about whether flow is controllable. Some view it as a lucky occurrence, others as a state well within their reach and one they can count on happening. Self-awareness and self-discipline are important foundations, as a triathlete describes, and components that are within our control:

> I think you can set it [flow] up. You can set the scene for it with all that preparation. It should be something that you can ask of yourself and get into, I think, through your training and through your discipline, because *you* have to be the one that reads your body.

Training the mind and the body are important, and as this quote demonstrates, knowing oneself is critical to preparing the way for flow experiences. Being aware of flow and the factors that lead to it allows athletes to be able to work toward optimal experiences.

Although it may seem that flow occurs independently of any direct input of your own, it may be that you are facilitating flow at a subconscious level by thoughts and actions prior to and during the event.

It is for this reason that some athletes occasionally resort to the kinds of behaviors that to outsiders seem to be nothing more than superstition. Ken Dryden, highly successful hockey goalie for the Montreal Canadiens, wrote about his life in hockey. In his acclaimed book *The Game*, he describes superstitious behaviors he came to rely on at different points in his career. For example, there was a particular usherette in the Forum, where home games were played, whom Dryden would smile and nod at in the warm-up: he associated that with winning after the sequence happened on one occasion before a personally successful performance in a game his team won. At another time, he followed a different routine:

> Before each game, I must take the first shot; it must strike the boards to the right of my net between the protective glass and the ice. If it doesn't, I will play poorly.

The highly analytical Dryden went on to explain how he used his superstitious behaviors to help him at game time:

I want to feel connected to what I do. I want the feelings a game gives unshared, undiminished by something separate from me. . . . I use it [superstition] as a focus for the fear I feel. Afraid of a bad game each time I play, I use Joyce and the first shot to distract me from the fear of a bad game, which I can't control, to the superstition, which I can.

Ballplayers might wear lucky charms or a favorite pair of shoes or grow beards in the hope of achieving a better performance. Some athletes will cross themselves before an event or go through the motions of some other personal ritual. If one expected such acts to produce an effect in some external, miraculous way, they would certainly amount to superstition. But if these behaviors help focus the athlete's mind and provide a sense of control over the activity, then they can actually serve the purpose of achieving the focus necessary to enter flow.

Sometimes in team sports one or more teammates can create a momentum that helps to bring about a team flow. Because so many more factors need to be right, team flow is more difficult to attain. Still, when it occurs, the team members all being in tune with one another, the performance can be a very special experience.

Flow allows athletes to fully partake in their sport, without holding back for fear of failure or embarrassment. Whether experienced by an individual athlete or a team, flow provides freedom from concerns that things may not work out. A figure skater discussed the term *flow* and the experience of abandon this state brought her:

A lot of people use the term *in sync*. I don't really like that. I don't know why. Or people say, "That was the performance of a lifetime," those types of things; they all seem so cliché. Flow doesn't sound cliché because the feeling isn't cliché, you know? The feeling is really wild, you feel like you completely abandon everything. You push harder than you ever push, you're not afraid that anything bad is going to happen.

This lack of fear, lack of restraint, is really what the feeling of control in flow is all about. Perceiving that everything is in place, that the task confronting us is doable, we can let go of all the inhibitions that make us timid and fearful in everyday life, and experience instead the freedom that flow provides.

Focusing on Fun

S port can be great fun—this is something you knew when you first took it up. In recent times when you have really enjoyed sport, what were the feelings? Probably words like fun, exhilaration, or excitement come to mind; you may remember laughing or smiling and feeling really good about yourself.

Fun and Flow

List the words that come to mind when you have fun at sport. Then compare your list with the words that athletes use to describe the flow state (see table 1.1). Are there terms in common? Often the words we use to describe the flow state are similar to those that describe fun.

Sport provides opportunities to release stress and tension, let go of worries, and become absorbed in the activity at hand. It can even produce a sense of spiritual fulfillment, of living on a level that is somehow more complete and harmonious than we are used to experiencing in everyday life.

ADMIT IT—IT'S FUN

Sport is a time to play, in contrast to the seriousness with which we lead our daily lives. We *play* sport, we don't *work* sport. However, often the playfulness of sport is lost and it becomes just another serious activity that provides little intrinsic enjoyment.

When children begin to take part in physical activities, they do so with a sense of play that sets the standard for what fun is. When adults take part in sport, it can be deadly serious. Reputations, hundreds of thousands of dollars, championship rings, careers, fame, and notoriety are at stake. Sport has become a highly commercialized and a highly political realm where many have much to gain or lose from the outcome of a game. Professional athletes are a part of a larger system, in which men and women with money and power are calling the shots. So where does this leave enjoyment in sport?

Most of us became involved in sport as games we played for fun with peers. The activities may not have made much sense outside of the sandlot, but they had special meaning to the players, because in the playing the mind and body came together in a seamless whole.

Most sports, to those who don't follow them, might seem rather strange, but for participants the shared sense of meaning derived from the rules of the activity creates clear goals and opportunities to demonstrate skills. What is the significance of getting an odd-shaped ball over a line drawn on a field? Or a spear-like instrument thrown as far as one is able? Football and javelin are very different events, but both can be analyzed from afar as possessing little inherent meaning. At least javelin can be traced back to hunting and gathering times, when having the ability to throw a spear long distances increased the chances of obtaining food for survival. This is not meant to belittle any sport activities, but to point out that the meaning of a sport depends on accepting the rules and challenges that define the event. To the historical meaning of a sport are added personal meanings that develop through participation and can become the driving force for athletes committed to excellence. We will explore these meanings a little further.

AUTOTELIC EXPERIENCES— THEIR OWN JUSTIFICATION

What prompts runners to venture out in all weather conditions nearly every day for their solo jaunts on roads, sidewalks, and tracks? What drives swimmers to spend countless hours alone in the pool trying to

© Claus Andersen

perfect their stroke and endurance? Writers for sport columns or TV broadcasts often focus on money, scholarships, medals, and fame—the rewards granted star athletes. But 99 percent of us play sports for other, much less tangible, reasons.

When we do something for the enjoyment it provides, instead of for some external reason that justifies the activity, the motivation is found within the activity, not externally. *Intrinsic motivation* describes getting involved or doing something for the love of it, with no expectation of future reward or gain. For those who invest their time and energies in sport, there is almost always an intrinsic factor present, at least in the beginning stages. For many people sport remains primarily an activity that is intrinsically rewarding, and few if any external factors form part of the reasons for participation. For others—and, ironically, this tends to be true of the most skilled athletes—the intrinsic reasons get lost amidst the sponsorship dollars, competition schedules, and training regimes. When sport becomes a business or a career, it loses some of its intrinsically motivating qualities as other reasons for participation move to the forefront. There is nothing wrong with defining sport as work rather than play, but when it is the former, the intrinsic qualities of sport may recede into the background or disappear altogether. One consequence of this is a potential loss of the enjoyment you can gain from the activity itself.

Flow is basically an autotelic experience, which is another way of denoting something that is intrinsically rewarding. As explained in chapter 1, the word *autotelic* comes from two Greek words meaning "self" and "goal." So autotelic activities are those that need no other justification because they have a built-in goal. The goal is simply to do the activity for its own sake, or, more precisely, for the experience it provides. Athletes can be playing sport for sheer enjoyment, that is, for autotelic reasons. Or money can motivate the participation, in which case there is an outside reason for taking part. Both reasons may be important at different stages of an athlete's career, and both intrinsic and extrinsic rewards may jointly provide the motivation. But trying to respond to both motivational sources can become quite a difficult balancing act, as autotelic and extrinsic rewards are quite different.

Why do you take part in sport? Think of as many reasons as you can, and write them in column 1 of table 9.1. In the second column, give a priority rating to each of these reasons. Give a "1" to a very important reason, a "2" to a somewhat important reason, and a "3" to a slightly important reason. Then, in column 3, work out whether the items listed in column 1 are intrinsic (I) or extrinsic (E) factors. If the reason has mostly to do with performing the activity and enjoying the feelings associated with it, more than likely it is an intrinsic factor. If the reason has more to do with things that come afterward—such as good health, powerful abductors, the approval of friends—it is likely to be an extrinsic factor. See how many I's and E's you have in column 3 and you will have some indication of how likely it is that you are experiencing flow.

One advantage of taking part in sport for intrinsic reasons is that you are likely to have a much better time with such an outlook. Your

Table 9.1		
What Motivates You?		
My reasons for taking part in sport	*Priority rating: 1, 2, or 3**	*Intrinsic (I) or extrinsic (E) motivation*
*Ratings: 1 = Very important reason, 2 = Somewhat important reason, 3 = Slightly important reason		

goals influence what you focus on. When the goal is to enjoy the sport, attention is directed toward the activity itself, as what is to be gained is found within the doing. When the goal is to obtain an external outcome, no longer is doing the activity for its own sake the focus. The athlete's attention is split between the activity and the desired external outcome, with the result that less psychic energy is left to monitor and execute the performance. And as the activity itself loses significance, so does the likelihood of experiencing flow from it.

This is why professionalism in sport has such an ambiguous reputation. Look at the deleterious effect of huge salaries and long-term contracts on the performance and attitude of many pro athletes. When sport becomes merely a means to a paycheck, intrinsic motives fall into the background, and sport's unique potential for creating enjoyment disappears.

It can be difficult to remain focused on the intrinsic aspects once the external rewards start to clamor for attention. Great coaches are able to bring their athletes back to focusing on what commands attention and draws an athlete to participating in the first place. Phil Jackson, coach of the highly successful Chicago Bulls of the 1990s, taught his players about becoming totally involved in the process of playing basketball. Explaining the shift in consciousness he tried to impart to his players as they came to play, Jackson wrote in his bestselling book, *Sacred Hoops*,

> Most rookies arrive in the NBA thinking that what will make them happy is having unlimited freedom to strut their egos on national TV. But that approach to the game is an inherently empty experience. What makes basketball so exhilarating is the joy of losing yourself completely in the dance, even if it's just for one beautiful transcendent moment.

SPORT AND COMPETENCE

Sport provides fine opportunities for demonstrating skills, and a path for continued development via the many defined levels of achievement. Most people are motivated to show that they are competent, and many find within sport the best opportunities for building skills and displaying proficiency. Matching skills against appropriate challenges is enjoyable, and sport provides excellent opportunities to stretch these levels to new heights.

The CS balance that defines flow can be readily achieved within sports and physical activities, and the opportunities to structure situations according to a personally defined CS balance are endless. The activities that qualify as sports make an enormous list, and it seems that new alternatives are being developed all the time. Not so long ago such sports as snowboarding, skydiving, or unassisted deep-sea diving did not exist.

Often new sports arise through combining aspects of different ones into a new event. One example that might not initially appear a likely package is unicycle hockey: add to the challenge of riding a unicycle the ball- and stick-handling skills of hockey and you have a new sport. There are many examples besides unicycle hockey of creating new sports from aspects of others already in existence: canoe polo, rhythmic diving, and triathlon are all hybrids of other sports, and there are many examples of new sports being created from adaptations or combinations of other activities. The content of a particular sport matters less than the opportunities it provides for demonstrating skills and finding challenge.

© The Picture Desk

Developing and demonstrating competence and having fun are two of the most important reasons for taking part in sport. These are the main rewards that account for intrinsic motivation, and both are precursors to flow, making sport a great context for optimal experiences. However, as much research has shown, when something that is enjoyable in itself begins to be rewarded from the outside, what was originally fun can turn into a chore. For instance, when children who love to paint are given gold stars or other prizes for their paintings, they begin to enjoy it less and do less of it—in part because they then sense that those who provide the rewards have taken control over the activity. The enjoyment of sport is similarly vulnerable to extrinsic rewards. We now look in more detail at overcoming some of the obstacles to enjoyment for sport participants.

KEYS TO ENJOYMENT

Analyzing enjoyment is a tricky process; it can diminish the fun that comes from the spontaneous excitement inherent in sports. The simple exhortation "Have fun" that we give and receive when we start an activity shows that we recognize the importance of enjoyment. But how do we translate that wish into practice? The fact is we cannot force ourselves to have fun. Nor can we force others. Enjoyment begins when all the obstacles are removed, and we become lost in the activity.

But there are ways to prepare the mind so that fun will come more readily. For instance, if you approach sport too seriously, if you can't occasionally see the humor of some of its aspects (say, the strange dedication of scarcely clad people pushing their bodies beyond the limits of endurance), you might also be missing some of its most joyful aspects. If you take stats and standings too seriously, if you can't lose gracefully, if every event is a do-or-die proposition, you risk missing the best that sport has to offer—release from the tyranny of external rewards and punishments. Sport is designed to be fun, and by remembering this we are more likely to enjoy it.

Watch Out for the Boomerangs

The desire to win, to be recognized as the best, and to secure a financial future are all reasonable motivations for competitive athletes. Each of these are outcomes or possible outcomes of successful performance. While they may be strong motivating factors during the heavy training and preparation period before an important event, they can be a distraction during the event. When what you consider most important lies in the future, the present can become simply a means of getting there. Yet it is in the present that flow is found, so if the present is disregarded in an attempt to ensure the future, the quality of the experience will certainly suffer. Of course the task must be completed before the goal is reached, but this can occur in a mindless fashion, where the present moment is nothing more than a time period to be passed through before the goal can eventually be obtained.

Outcomes of sport are extrinsic factors, and they come in many forms. They may be obvious things, such as winning or prize money. Less obvious but no less significant are the motivations of recognition or acceptance that drive many athletes to keep performing well.

Wanting to lose weight or increase cardiovascular fitness are also extrinsic motivators that keep some people chained to an exercise program. Whatever the reason, if enjoyment is not part of the picture, a great opportunity for improving life will be lost.

Remembering what provides the most enjoyment helps you to increase sport's intrinsic rewards. It may be the sense of speed and power you feel during sprint events or the feel of sailing in a strong wind. The ability to move the body in space in difficult maneuvers is fun for many gymnasts and divers. Eye-hand or eye-foot coordination is an enjoyable skill to master and is central to ball sports such as tennis, football, and basketball. Learning to master the skills of a sport brings tremendous satisfaction. To be able to increase the level of challenge and match this with your skills is something unique to sport, and a source of deep exhilaration.

Sometimes athletes and coaches are involved in sport without really knowing why they are doing it. It is worth thinking about the aspects that provide you with a sense of challenge and enjoyment. If you learn to focus more attention on these aspects, it will be easier to maintain motivation because you will enjoy what you are doing more.

A world-class figure skater, describing a final performance before retiring from amateur skating, spoke about what she wanted to experience when she took to the ice:

> I wasn't thinking when I got on the ice [that] I want to skate well so that the money contracts come in or so that people think I'm a great skater, or that everybody thinks, "Well, she has really ended her career on a high note." I wanted to skate well because I've never felt flow to the nth degree. I've always felt good but I really wanted to feel something [more]. . . . When I got on that ice I was scared, but I felt there was something powerful that I desired, a feeling of satisfaction, of giving it all and getting it all back, and pleasing and making everybody happy, but pleasing myself. . . . I wasn't thinking, I'm going to really entertain this audience. I thought of key points in the program that I enjoyed performing.

Focusing on the performance to the exclusion of everything else paid off for this skater. It was a performance she remembers as being the most satisfying in her career.

Turn Competition Into Play

For many athletes, competition is fun. It is a chance to test yourself against others as well as against yourself. Because the stakes are higher

© Robert Oliver

in competition than in practice, athletes often prefer the time of competition. We discussed in chapter 5 (on goals) the advantages of holding a task orientation while competing. It is important to remember that a task orientation involves much more than focusing on performing well. For the swimmer, it includes paying attention to the silvery stream of water around the body; for the climber, it involves caressing the rock until one feels through one's fingertips the ancient bones of the mountain.

To enjoy a sport one doesn't have to win at it or even do well. Some of the most enduring memories of physical activity may refer to painful, disastrous moments when the athlete first understood something important about her strengths and limitations or about the elements of her sport. A sailor whose boat sprung a leak during a long-distance race had to bail water for days without interruption until she came in sight of harbor, but when she set foot on the dock, she was a different person from the one who had set sail a week before. The task she conquered was almost inhuman in its demands, but she met the challenge successfully, and probably never felt as much flow before or after as she did during those wet and miserable days.

The more a person learns to love the details of the sport, the more easily he will get lost in the task. Even lacing one's athletic shoes, if done as a personal ritual, can help focus one's mind on what is to come. The smells of a gym are not usually considered on a par with the finest perfumes, but if the gymnast or ball player pays attention to them and associates pleasant memories with them, the first whiff of gym smell will help the mind concentrate. The feel of a bike's handlebars, the heft of a climber's carabiner, the smooth movement of the oars for the rower—these are only a few of the hundreds of elements that an athlete can learn to appreciate, and that will help to focus the mind. They will keep attention on the activity, and this present-centeredness will facilitate the absorption that leads to flow.

Competition is also a strong source of motivation that helps maintain focus. But when winning is all that matters, and what happens in the process becomes of secondary importance, competition becomes a distraction. Just as with an outcome orientation, competition can lessen the importance of the process in the minds of participants. Since the process is where the enjoyment originates, devaluing it can take away from the joy of sport.

Rebalance Challenges and Skills

The total concentration that the merging of action and awareness requires is disrupted when the CS balance is missing. If the climb becomes too easy, the climber begins to be distracted because he senses that paying full attention to the rock and the moves is no longer necessary. As attention begins to wander, the usual concerns and worries begin to appear in the mind, and the enjoyment of the climb is disrupted. A similar scenario unfolds in the opposite case, when the climb threatens to become too difficult for the climber's ability: now the concerns about falling or having to spend a chilling night on the mountain interfere with the experience.

In team sports, it is sometimes difficult to maintain the right balance because what is the right level of challenge for one person might be too much for someone less skilled, or too little for someone whose abilities are greater. For instance if you are climbing with a real pro, he might be enjoying the pitch while you are out of your mind with anxiety. If you are an intermediate skier, it might be difficult to refuse following your more experienced friend down an expert slope, because you might lose face in the process. Peer pressure is one of the extrinsic factors that often interferes with the enjoyment of an athletic activity.

Maintaining an appropriate CS balance is an ongoing task that both athlete and coach should pay attention to in order to keep what they are doing enjoyable. It is a balancing act in sport, as the challenges cannot all be predicted in advance and many factors affect our perceptions of ability. Having flexibility in how you view things and being adaptable to changing demands are skills that facilitate keeping the doors open to flow experiences.

Remember that the CS balance is a subjective ratio. In other words, some individuals feel in balance when their actual skills are somewhat higher than the objective difficulties, while others concentrate most when the challenges are somewhat higher than their objective skills. It is important to find out where your point of optimal dynamic balance lies, and to learn to stay there, varying the levels of challenges as needed.

ENJOYMENT IN FLOW

Although an athlete in flow might be too busy to notice it during the performance, enjoyment is often the most well-remembered and treasured aspect of the experience. Simon describes the lift to the athlete that flow provides:

> That is what gives you the buzz to keep doing what you're doing, to keep doing the sport. Because once you've done it, once you've got it, then it just lifts you. Once you lose it, it can be a real slog till you've got it back again. And once you've got it back and you're just grooving along, everything is going well, that's great. That's just what you want it to be.

Once experienced, flow becomes like a magnetic pole that pulls us toward it. The feelings that flow provides can be some of the most treasured of all our experiences. Athletes who have been there, who have experienced flow, know what these athletes we've cited in this book are experiencing:

> My body feels great. . . . You feel as though you just can't be beaten at anything. You're on top of the world, nothing else can bring you down. It was amazing. I was on a high after that game for ages. It is an amazing feeling.

> Each jump I hit it was like I was riding a wave. My confidence grew as the program went on. I didn't feel tired. I enjoyed it immensely. It was wonderful. It is what all the hard work over the years is about.

Linked with this amazing feeling often is superior performance. So flow experiences are often peak experiences, as this runner recalls: "I really enjoyed the experience of running and really had probably the most successful race of my life." It is not surprising that when everything is optimal in the athlete's mind, the body produces outstanding performance. However, remember the experience, for ultimately it is how much we enjoy rather than how much we gain or achieve that matters. Flow is so special because everything comes together and feels perfect during it. We remember this feeling, and it becomes the standard of what life should be always.

Where to From Here?

In many ways, civilization consists of finding ways to feel better. We see evidence that ever since the beginnings of human history people have tried to improve the quality of their experiences by various means. They have done it by swallowing chemical substances, like psychedelic mushrooms or fermented liquors. They have done it through music, dance, and ritual ceremonies. In the past few centuries, at least, they have done it in part through participation in organized sports and athletics. Different as these practices are from each other, they have the common purpose of creating subjective psychological states that are more desirable than what we are likely to experience in the routines of everyday life.

It is certain that as we move into the future, techniques for improving the quality of life will continue to develop. New forms will emerge, and old forms will change. And given the fact that technologies and the lifestyles they support have gone through an exponential explosion in the recent past, the kinds of things people will be doing to create flow in their lives will presumably be different from what they are now. What is the future of sport as we enter the third millennium?

DEVELOPING NEW KINDS OF SPORT

There are two main directions that are interesting to think about. The first is simply the discovery of new ways to use the potentialities of the body in a challenging context—in other words, the emergence of new sports. The enormous variety of sports we now take for granted dates only from the past hundred or so years, and few sports go back more than two centuries. It is true that villagers in the Middle Ages used to compete in archery, in throwing boulders, or in foot-races and that athletes competed in Olympic and other games in ancient Greece. But these were more communal ceremonies than the kind of individual sport events we are familiar with now. As long as most people labored in the fields from dawn to dusk or slogged from one battlefield to the next, there was no great need of additional physical exercise.

Sports as we know them now began to be formalized only after the Industrial Revolution reached its peak. In a matter of a few decades around the middle of the last century most sports—from golf to tennis, from baseball to soccer—became formally organized with rules, uniforms, and competing leagues. And new sports have emerged at a feverish rate ever since. Especially in the United States, these games have tended to be highly individualized and relatively unstructured, depending on personal skills and decisions: consider, for example, surfing, hang-gliding, snowboarding, rock climbing, scuba diving, or mountain biking.

Traditional sports tend to have simple goals, summarized in the Olympic motto "Higher, faster, stronger." The newer sports tend to be more sophisticated, relying more on style, uniqueness, and imagination. More formal, competitive forms have also emerged, emphasizing endurance and a variety of skills, from mass marathon runs to Ironman events. Another recent development has been the forming of rules and leagues for special populations, such as seniors or people with disabilities.

We might expect that as our lifestyles continue to become more and more sedentary and predictable, new sports that rely on effort and risk will emerge so that we do not lose entirely the kind of flow experiences that the use of the body can provide. As in the past, new forms are likely to emerge from groups of young people with time on their hands who are reluctant to settle down into routine occupations. Consider the Colorado "ski bums" who took up hot-dogging, mogul skiing, and snowboarding or residents of the beach communities in California, Australia, and Hawaii where surfing was first developed.

It can only be frustrating to attempt to predict the future in fine detail. Few people have a decent record at guessing what the world will look like 20, 10, or even 5 years down the line. Human beings are too ingenious, and social forces too complex, for us to foresee what things will look like in the future. It is true that an occasional few individuals hit the mark with their prognostications. For instance, in 1963 Philip Knight wrote a paper for a college assignment in which he described what he thought was an important lifestyle change just then appearing over the horizon: an increasing interest in personal health and physical fitness. He believed that an increasing number of ordinary people would want to emulate professional athletes, and that if one were to produce and market equipment formerly designed for elite sportsmen, it would have a mass appeal. A few years later he and W.J. Bowerman, his running coach, merged their modest savings and began to experiment with a line of athletic shoes. Twelve years later, their new company, Nike, was worth more than $400 million. In the process Nike also contributed to the very change it took advantage of, by promoting a lifestyle of vigorous physical activity.

There will always be visionaries like Philip Knight, who correctly anticipate a trend in the making. But visionaries are few and far between. Nevertheless, even pedestrian prognosticators like us can make a few educated guesses. The potentialities of the human body will continue to provide the basis for flow experiences. The limits of what nerves and muscles can do will be expanded. The elements in which the body can act—air (gliding, bungee jumping, sky diving), water (swimming, surfing, diving), and earth (running, climbing, spelunking) will continue offering unimagined opportunities for action. But advances in knowledge and technology will provide new tools for interaction, just as did the bicycle, the oxygen tank, or athletic diets after their introduction in the recent past. We hope this will never happen, but one cannot exclude the possibility that through genetic engineering it will be possible to manufacture bodies with exceptional physical attributes—a superior cardiovascular system or the ability to clear tall buildings with a single leap.

The trend toward ever more customized challenges geared to individualized skills is likely to gather an even greater momentum. People will still specialize in such things as fishing in the Alaskan wilderness, helicopter skiing in the Canadian Rockies or the New Zealand Alps, exploring sections of the Great Barrier or the Belize reefs, and developing refined skateboarding techniques. Technology will open up opportunities for space walks and undersea explorations.

But because few individuals are content to receive purely individual feedback to measure their achievements, these emergent sports will also need a social context that provides respect and admiration for individual achievements. Therefore, small groups of specialists will form around these new opportunities. Leagues and associations will spring up, not in the attempt to develop nationwide networks but to produce more intimate, boutique-like operations, such as the commercial climbing outfits that offer clients Himalayan expeditions or guided ascents to the Seven Summits.

Three constraints will shape the future of sports: The first includes the limitations of the physical body and its physical environment. The second and more creative component includes new developments in our knowledge of biology and in the technological extensions of human action through tools and equipment. And the third shaping force consists of the limitations of the social and cultural environment. For instance, if we encounter another great economic recession, few people will be able to afford to fish in Alaska or exercise in space. It is out of this mix of factors that new forms of experiencing flow through sport will arise.

VIRTUAL SPORTS

One of the most frequently asked questions about flow is something that could be summarized as "But what happens inside the brain during flow?" The reason for people asking this question is that many of us believe that our feelings are directly controlled by chemical changes in the nervous system, such as fluctuating levels of adrenaline or endorphins. A natural consequence of this belief in chemical influences is thinking that flow is nothing more than a chemical process, and we'll therefore soon be in a position to induce it directly by changing brain chemistry through drugs or through genetic engineering. Then years spent in training and tens of thousands of dollars to get the exhilaration of climbing Mount Everest won't be necessary; we'll be able to get the same feeling lying on a couch and sucking a pill.

This belief has a strong foundation in fact. It is true that every feeling we experience is accompanied by discrete chemical changes in the nervous system. It is true that when we feel we are in danger, part of the brain releases an extra dose of adrenaline. Things become more complicated, however, in knowing precisely what causes what. As any first-year statistics student knows, "correlation does not imply causation." And this truism is a particularly apt warning when mental processes are involved.

It is difficult, for instance, to disentangle the role of mental images from their physiological consequences. If John gets a strong jolt of adrenaline skiing down a particular run and Mary does not, is it because John's hormones flow more freely or because John is more afraid of that particular run, perhaps because he heard about some friend who took a bad spill skiing down that very slope? So what is the distinct contribution, on the one hand, of our physiological hardware and, on the other, of the software of mental images we create and endow with meaning?

The effects of drugs similarly depend on the mental environment in which their chemistry takes place. If an American Indian shaman chews peyote in a traditional cultural setting, he may get a positive experience of illumination from it; but the same peyote may induce the screaming meemies in someone unequipped to handle it. There is no *direct* effect from the chemical on experience: The physiological change must be interpreted to produce a feeling. The same dose of the same drug may make one feel relatively good at one time and miserable at another.

There was a time not so long ago, for instance, when a lot of media hype proclaimed that psychedelic drugs help a person to be creative and to liberate the mind. Yet there does not seem to be any real evidence that anyone came up with a new idea or product as the result of altering consciousness chemically. Certainly many writers get drunk before or after they sit down to write, but the real work of putting words together on a page requires a sober mind. A dull person will remain dull even after ingesting a ton of hallucinogens; a creative person can do great work stone sober.

The point is that when we give up control of consciousness to an outside agency, the virtual experience is never the same as the natural one. This is especially true of sport. A sport event is never complete in the moment in which it takes place. Much of its rewards come afterward, when a person thinks back on what she has accomplished. The flow of sport extends to the feeling of having created flow through hard work. Without having coped with real challenges, the experience lacks a vital ingredient.

So suppose that somehow we learn to replicate the flow of a hang glider by recreating exactly the physiological state of her brain during the glide. And suppose now that we "play back" these chemical patterns on the brain of a person sitting in a dark room. Will the flow experience of the person sitting in the room be the same as that of the original glider? We can be confident that it will not. First, unless one has been involved in gliding for some time, many of the dimensions of the experience will be meaningless and uninteresting to the person in the room. He might have the exact same feelings as the original model, but they will not *mean* the same thing, because he will not be able to associate them with prior experiences and knowledge. More importantly, while the natural glider will be able to savor the experience later as something she made happen, the virtual glider will know that he has been merely a consumer, rather than a creator, of the experience.

It is quite certain that virtual sport has a future—as many other forms of vicarious experience have had, from recorded music to television. People will be able to sit alone in a booth and see the great wall of Lhotse raise above the Western Cwm, feel the frigid winds of Everest blowing by, hear the scrunch of the crampons on the ice, and labor to breathe in the thin atmosphere. Most of these viewers will lose their appetite, vomit uncontrollably, and have splitting headaches. The virtual experience might be organized so that only one in 20 attempts will actually reach the summit. One in six persons may actually "die" in a fall or an avalanche, and several will "lose" their fingers to frostbite. Those who make it to the summit will certainly get a sense of pride in having reached the top, the same kind that people now experience winning a close chess game or in stopping the evil scientist who created "Riven" in the popular computer game. But will this be still a sport?

No, neither chemistry nor electronics will replace the natural high that the direct use of the body can give. Overcoming physical challenges, stretching the capacity of sinew and lung, running real risks of pain, failure, and even death—these are the constituents of sport, and as long as people are people, they will continue to provide a kind of flow that is unique to human beings. It is an optimal experience tailored by millions of years of slow evolution, and one that in the future will lead us to ever higher plateaus in experiencing deeper the potentialities of the body. But for it to be all that it can be, sport will have to keep involving the whole person: willpower, courage, and imagination, as well as orchestrating a full symphony of feelings in the physical body. To imagine that the flow of sport can be passively experienced is to completely misunderstand what sport is—and what flow is.

GETTING CLOSER TO FLOW NATURALLY

We have written this book to help make sport experiences more enjoyable and to identify the key characteristics that make them so. We hope that by understanding flow better, people will get the full depth of psychic rewards that sport can offer. But can this special state be called upon at will? Whether flow can ever be a controllable state is a question of interest to athletes, coaches, and sport psychologists. That is, if the necessary conditions are in place, will flow occur? If you accept our argument that achieving flow through chemical or virtual means is not the optimal way to approach this question, then we should ask what athletes and coaches can do to help make the flow experience attainable and repeatable.

Setting the stage for flow by mastering its known components is a positive step toward increasing its occurrence. Training the mind and the body are important, and having self-awareness is critical to preparing the way. Being aware of flow and the factors that lead to it allows athletes to slip into the right frame of mind. When the factors are in place, some athletes feel that nothing will stop them from becoming lost in the experience. What are these factors? In writing this book, we have purposefully held back from presenting something like the "12 steps to flow." Instead we have described factors that enhance flow and those that make it less likely to occur, using examples from athletes in many sports. It is impossible to give a generic recipe. First, each person's interests and skills are slightly different from those of everyone else. Second, if you follow a set of instructions worked out by someone else, you will never be entirely in control of your experience. Recipes are all right for learning how to bake a cake, but they don't work for learning how to achieve harmony in consciousness. That is something you have to discover on your own, by applying the general principles of flow to your own situation.

Flow is found by listening to your inner voice, which can tell you what your true interests are; by developing the skills necessary to become immersed in a challenging activity; by learning to focus on concrete goals and on subtle feedback. However, flow is not guaranteed. It is not a state of mind that can be manufactured and distributed in packaged form. Like the aesthetic experience one has when confronting great music or great art, it is a delicate process that must be individually created. In sport, it develops through years of disciplined training, and it might take a different form for any given athlete. Following certain guidelines will help, but the right steps will vary for different individuals in different sports.

A rower described flow as a "little bit of magic" and explained how one could set the stage for it, but could not guarantee the experience:

> I think you can improve the chance of it happening . . . but it is a little bit of magic, like, that is why we say that you can't really describe it or guarantee it or anything. I think it is definitely a little bit setting the stage, if you like, for trying to make it happen. I think it is what you are looking for all the time.

The description of flow as having a magical quality alludes to its elusive character. It is not an easy state to achieve; it demands energy and self-confidence, these often in the face of great difficulty. But sometimes we are surprised by experiencing flow unexpectedly, seemingly without any effort, as a rugby player describes:

> For me, it [flow] is something that is almost totally dependent upon my preparation. Most of the times I've achieved that state have been through my own controlling it. But sometimes, just the pure action of what happened in the game, I had no influence on. And that's what I mean, sometimes you have control over it, but at certain times you don't need to have any input; you're just there, and you're taken along with it.

While not all the factors can be controlled, many can. You probably have a good understanding of what flow is by this point, and you will have your own experiences to draw on. What does Simon have to say about controlling flow?

> I believe the flow state can be a controllable thing. Someone who can control it has got a lot of power in the sport. I think I know how to get it, but it takes a lot of practice. And a lot of work. And you have to master these things in your head.

Simon rated himself about halfway there to being able to control flow, realizing there were many challenges to be met before this optimal state could be called on at will. He went on to attribute his present status in his sport to his ability to get in touch with flow, and the flow experiences he had attained were treasured in memory, to help him return to this state in the future.

Once the goal is clear, the path to its attainment also becomes clearer. If the goal is to achieve an optimal experience, knowing what it is you are trying to achieve is critical and will start you on the journey.

THE IMPORTANCE OF POSITIVE EXPERIENCES

When we first start to run, bike, or play basketball, we do it because it's fun. We don't need any psychologist to explain why we should do it: the feeling we get is a good enough reason. Later, we may continue the activity because, in addition to experiencing sheer physical exhilaration, we enjoy being with friends, want to learn new skills, or feel the kick of competition. Still later we may do sport primarily to stay in shape or for health reasons. But if we lose the enjoyment that initially hooked us on sport, we run the risk of missing the whole point.

Yet, unfortunately, this loss is often the case. Many people keep running or biking out of a sense of duty or bitter resolution, having long lost the joy they initially experienced. Bad coaching, excessive competition, and boring sport bureaucracies take their toll. Adolescents typically report very positive moods when taking part in sport. However, young athletes drop out of sport in increasing numbers. Many teenagers drop out when sport is no longer fun. Attrition also occurs in exercise programs, and here the number of dropouts is even higher than for sports. Despite the fact that exercise makes us healthy and fit, it is difficult to keep to a physical regimen if we don't like to do it. So the quality of the experience is a critical factor in compliance with any sport activity.

EXTENDING YOUR GOAL STILL FURTHER

There is an ancient Chinese curse that says "May you reach all your goals." At first sight, one might wonder why such a wish could be considered a curse. Doesn't all of life consist in striving to reach some goal, whether money, fame, sexual satisfaction, or comfort? Isn't this what life is about? Well, yes and no. Goals are necessary to get us focused and going, but reaching them does not necessarily bring happiness or satisfaction. It is the journey that counts, not getting to the destination. This is true for life in general: more and more studies show that health, wealth, power, and fame do not make people happy; whereas those who learn to enjoy whatever they are doing, whether it brings them closer to their goals or not, end up having a meaningful and enjoyable life.

What is true for life as a whole is also true in the more limited domain of sport. Winning, getting medals, improving one's time, or beating a record are important to get us motivated at the beginning, but if we take these goals too seriously—so that their pursuit blinds us to the experience along the way—then we miss the main gift that sport can give.

Often reaching the peak of athletic excellence can leave one feeling puzzled and empty. When we see athletes who have reached the pinnacle of their sport, we tend to assume that they must have found the secret of enjoyment once and for all, and that they are proud indeed of what they have attained. Often this is true, but getting to the top can also be anticlimactic. In such a case, when doing sport is no longer enjoyable, the athlete experiences a "dark night of the soul" similar to that of artists who run out of ideas or religious persons who lose their faith. A triathlete who had been a world champion for a long time describes a sense of inner emptiness after she reached the very top:

> You never ever look at any performance . . . as being exceptional. You try and think, well that was good, but everything ultimately is a letdown. To me, there's always something that is more challenging. . . . I will never be satisfied with anything I do athletically . . . everything's so anticlimactic. You know, you train for weeks, months for an event, and it all seems so consuming and so important at the time, and every minute of every day you keep thinking about the event and your competitors. And then it's almost, Big Deal! The world didn't change, you're still the same person, and even though . . . I use financial rewards to motivate me sometimes, money will never bring happiness, so it's not like at the end of the day, Well, great, I won some money. . . . I always get more of a low. It's like, "Whoa, what am I going to do now?"

Even reaching the summit of a sport is eventually disillusioning if it is the world record that keeps one motivated, instead of the quality of the experience. This athlete had spoken positively about her flow experiences; when asked how important flow was to her continued involvement, this was her response:

> I couldn't do it if I didn't think I was going to get enjoyment from it again, and I constantly strive and strive to get to that state [flow]. . . . You can sort of recall how you felt in the event, running along thinking, "I'm happy to be alive, and this is great, and this is wonderful." So I pursue that, because I don't see the point of not loving what I do anymore. . . . I strive to get to that state of perfection.

Whether you are a rank amateur or a world champion, the ultimate measure of success is not your performance stats but what you were able to feel while performing. Someone who comes in first without having experienced the exhilaration of the race is to be pitied as much as the winner of the lottery who cannot get any pleasure from his millions. But being able to get flow from sport, whether in victory or defeat, is one sure way to make life richer. The intensity of the experience provides glimpses of perfection and beckons us to continue the search for excellence.

notes

Chapter 1

Authors' note. The quotations from athletes in this chapter and through-out the book, unless otherwise stated, come from research conducted by the authors. Relevant research by the authors and others whose work has a bearing on understanding flow, as well as quotations from other sources, are cited in this section. Complete references are provided in the bibliography at the end of this book.

page

4 **Olympic games of the ancient Greeks to the Mayan ball games.** A contemporary anthropological account of the Olympic games can be found in Mac Aloon, J. (1981). The Mayan ballgames were described in Csikszentmihalyi, M. and Bennett, S. (1971).

5 **Flow is a state with universal qualities.** For more information about the contexts in which flow has been studied, the reader is referred to other books by Csikszentmihalyi. For example, an edited volume by Csikszentmihalyi, M. and Csikszentmihalyi, I. (1988) contains accounts of flow across a number of different settings and cultures. *Flow* (1990) and *Finding Flow* (1997) provide comprehensive accounts of how the experience manifests itself in different aspects of our lives.

6 **Experience Sampling Method (ESM) responses.** This approach to studying human experiences in different life activities involves the wearing of pagers that are preprogrammed to go off at several times throughout the day. Once beeped, the respondent completes a short inventory of his or her activity, thoughts, and feelings at the time. For a more complete description of the ESM approach, see writings such as Csikszentmihalyi and Larson (1987) and Csikszentmihalyi, Rathunde, and Whalen (1993).

8 **Order in their consciousness.** In ordinary life, people typically experience conflict in consciousness. For example, an office worker might be sitting at his desk and adding up numbers, with part of his attention focused on the job and part of it focused on his wish to be out with his girlfriend. He resents having to sit, to be indoors, to work on his task. By contrast, in the flow state a person's subjective states are in harmony; the body and mind are working together without internal conflict. This state of ordered consciousness is one of the main rewards of the flow experience. When consciousness is in a state of inner conflict, we may speak of its *psychic entropy*, because thoughts and actions are disordered and less efficient. The flow or optimal experience, on the other hand, is a state of *psychic negentropy*, because the mind is efficient and internally harmonious.

11 **In the zone**. This popular term for moments in sport when everything comes together for the athlete has been the subject of inquiry for a number of authors. Notable examples are *Playing in the Zone* by Cooper (1998), *In the Zone* by Murphy and White (1995), and *The Achievement Zone* by Murphy (1996). These accounts of experience in the zone are substantially identical to what we call the flow experience.

11 **To distinguish flow from similar concepts**. In Jackson's (1992b) doctoral research, she asked elite athletes to describe their views of the similarities and differences between flow, peak performance, and peak experience. Whereas the elite athlete sample saw these experiences occurring together more often than independently, differences between the phenomena were also recognized. McInman and Grove (1991) discuss issues related to the different terms used to describe optimal moments in sport.

11 **Abraham Maslow** (1968) developed a theory of self-actualization to explain how people live and behave. Peak experiences are moments of self-actualization in process when the person is living to his or her highest potential and experiences a number of very positive characteristics, including unity and fulfillment.

13 **Complexity**. The concept of complexity is useful to describe what happens in evolution—at the biological as well as the psychological and cultural levels. When a system (an organism, a person, or a family) is both more *differentiated* and at the same time more *integrated* than another, we would say the first one is more complex than the second. For example, a person who develops unique skills, who thinks for herself, and who is independent and autonomous (i.e., is more differentiated) and who also forms strong relationships, participates in the community, and has internalized the knowledge of the culture (i.e., is more integrated) is more complex. Individual growth and development tends toward greater complexity, just as cultural evolution does. For more information about complexity see Csikszentmihalyi (1993).

Chapter 2

15 **Studies of peoples' optimal experiences**. Csikszentmihalyi's (1975) *Beyond Boredom and Anxiety* details the results of research with people from a wide array of contexts, including artists, surgeons, chess players, and athletes. Despite the large differences in the types of activities these groups of people were engaged in, there was a remarkable similarity in their experiences in the flow state. Jackson's (1992a, 1995, 1996) research with athletes has found remarkable consistency in the flow experience in sport.

16 **Fundamental components of flow**. The primary dimensions of flow have been developed by Csikszentmihalyi and are further described in his books, *Beyond Boredom and Anxiety* (1975), *Flow* (1990), *Creativity* (1996), and *Finding Flow* (1997). For athletes' descriptions of these flow dimensions, see Jackson's (1996) article, "Toward a Conceptual Understanding of the Flow Experience in Elite Athletes."

Chapter 3

35 **You always miss 100 percent of the shots you don't take.** Source is an inspirational print entitled "Opportunity," in *Successories of Illinois*, 1994.

38 **Pleasure of homeostasis.** Food, sex, and comfort provide some of the most pleasurable experiences in life, but the satisfaction of these needs does not lead to higher levels of complexity in individual development. The rewards of pleasure result from restoring a homeostatic balance of bodily needs, whereas enjoyment results from the use of learned skills that leads to the mastery of new challenges (Csikszentmihalyi 1990, pp. 45–48).

39 **Jon Krakauer** (1997) described his Everest experience in an enthralling book, *Into Thin Air*. This quote comes from p. 20.

42 **Dennis Rodman.** Source of Dennis Rodman quote is an article by Phil Taylor (1996) entitled, "The Trade," *Sports Illustrated*, 84 (9): 33.

43 **They are much happier when they do sport.** Sources of data for American teenagers and involvement in different activities are Csikszentmihalyi, M., and Larson, R. (1986); Csikszentmihalyi, M., Rathunde, K., and Whalen, S. (1993).

44 **Consequences of failing in athletics.** Failing in athletics can equate to failing as a person for those athletes who perceive themselves strongly, if not exclusively, through their role as athlete. Sport psychologists have studied the effects of having a strong athletic identity. See, for example, Brewer, Van Raalte, and Linder (1993), who argued that there are both positive and negative consequences to having a strong athletic identity.

44 **Jack Nicklaus** quote is from *The Edge* by Howard Ferguson (1986, pp. 5–54). This book contains many inspiring quotes from great athletes and coaches.

56 **Thought stopping.** To learn more about mental techniques for thought stopping, positive self-talk, and other means of building confidence in sport, see, for example, Zinsser, Bunker, and Williams (1998).

58 **Simulation training.** Just as pilots practice in flight simulators when they are learning to fly, athletes can benefit from going through competitive simulations of upcoming events. These can either cover aspects of performance or be full-scale dress rehearsals of a major performance.

59 The **confidence factor** is often the more critical of the two axes. Jackson and Roberts (1992) and Jackson, Kimiecik, Ford, and Marsh (1998) show that confidence, or perceived ability, is critical to the experience of flow in athletes.

59 **Nothing breeds success like success.** In his theory of self-efficacy, Bandura (1977) suggests that performance accomplishments are a major source of self-efficacy, the belief that one can successfully accomplish a task.

Chapter 4

69 **Non-optimal environments.** Themes encompassing obstacles presented by the sport environment as well as by people interacting with the athletes made up this category of responses about factors that athletes perceived as disrupting flow. This finding and other factors influencing flow are addressed

in Jackson's (1995) article, "Factors Influencing the Occurrence of Flow in Elite Athletes."

73 **What Zen monks try to achieve**. For a brief discussion of Yoga and Buddhist practices and flow see Csikszentmihalyi 1990, pp. 103–106, and 1993, pp. 45 ff. and 160 ff.

74 **Donovan Bailey** quote is from a story entitled "Toward 2000" in Ansett's in-flight magazine, *Panorama* (1998).

75 **Peter Croft**. Mike Randolph (1997) wrote a story on the awesome Canadian solo rock climber, Peter Croft. This quote comes from p. 52 of "On the Edge," in *Outdoor Canada*, May, 1997.

Chapter 5

77 **Having free time is not enough**. For instance Veroff, J., Douvan, E., and Kulka, R.A. (1981) reported that 49 percent of employed men claim that their work is more satisfying than leisure, whereas only 19 percent say that leisure is more satisfying than work. See also D.G. Myers (1992), *The Pursuit of Happiness*.

82 **Achievement goals**. Duda (1992) presents a good overview of the different types of goals in sport. Research by Jackson and Roberts (1992) has shown that task goals are related to competitive athletes' experiencing flow.

83 **Goals are the building blocks of motivation**. There is a plentiful research on the positive effects of goal setting on sport performance and on the principles of effective goal setting. See for example the overview chapter by Gould, D. (1998).

87 **Power of determination**. Quote from Roger Bannister taken from *The Edge* by Howard Ferguson (1986), pp. 2–22.

Chapter 6

93 **Psychologists who study happiness**. In the last decades the study of happiness, which for a long time was considered too "soft" a topic for serious scientists, has finally gained acceptance as an appropriate field for research. See for instance Inglehart, R. (1990); Myers, D. and Diener, E. (1995); Parducci, A. (1995); Veenhoven, R. (1988).

101 **How successfully the team can interconnect**. The importance of positive team relationships and communications, both on and off the field, was heard in interviews with team athletes conducted by Jackson (1992a, 1995).

102 **Coaches are a powerful source of communication**. Communicating effectively is a dynamic process that depends on a number of personal and situational variables. Dave Yukelson, sport psychologist at Penn State University, has written a practical guide in a chapter titled "Communicating Effectively" in Williams (1998). See also Thompson (1993).

105 **Without self-awareness an athlete misses important cues**. Ken Ravizza, sport psychologist to a number professional athletes and teams, discusses the importance of self-awareness to performance in his chapter, "Increasing Awareness for Sport Performance," in Williams (1998).

106 **Peter Croft** quote is from Mike Randolph (1997), p. 28.

Chapter 7

109 **Undivided attention is hard to come by**. Several studies have shown that everyday life activities usually involve a splitting of attention between several tasks and goals; see Csikszentmihalyi and Csikszentmihalyi (1988).

115 **Plan for the competition**. For further information on preparing competition plans, see Terry Orlick's (1986a, b) *Psyching for Sport* and *Coaches' Training Manual to Psyching for Sport*, which provide comprehensive coverage of mental preparation for competition.

118 **Powers of concentration**. To learn more about improving concentration skills, see Nideffer (1989) who developed a detailed approach for developing attentional abilities in sport.

123 **The concept of Yu**. The similarities between the Chinese concept of *Yu* and flow were first pointed out by W. Sun (1987), *Flow and Yu: Comparison of Csikszentmihalyi's theory and Chuang-tzu's philosophy*.

Chapter 8

128 **Strong feelings of control**. Jackson's (1992a, 1995) interview-based research with elite athletes found that many individuals reported perceiving they were in control during flow.

133 **Optimal energy zone**. For a review of sport psychology research on optimal energy and arousal, see Jones, G., and Hardy, L. (1990). Yuri Hanin (1995) describes zones of optimal performance, which depend on individual optimal levels of arousal, described as zones of optimal functioning.

138 **Ken Dryden** wrote a very thoughtful and analytical book (1989) on his experiences as a champion ice hockey player. This quote comes from pp. 215- 216 of *The Game*.

Chapter 9

143 **Intrinsic motivation**. Deci and Ryan (1985) have studied intrinsic motivation for many years and have developed a theory of why it works. The concept of self-determination, or feeling in control of one's actions, is central to their theory.

146 **Phil Jackson's** (1995) *Sacred Hoops* is an outstanding account of a coach who has been highly successful at helping his athletes to play in the moment. This quote is from p. 91 of his chapter entitled "Selflessness in Action."

147 **Developing and demonstrating competence and having fun**. These are two of the most important motives for sport participation. To learn more about research on the motives behind sport participation, see Weiss and Chaumeton (1992).

150 **Enduring memories of physical activity may refer to painful, disastrous moments**. This account of a sailor's ordeal is found in Knox-Johnston's (1969), *A World of My Own*.

Epilogue

156 **Villagers in the Middle Ages used to compete in archery**. For a history of how various sports like archery developed in their social context, see Kelly (1982).

157 **Visionaries like Philip Knight**. Silver (1985, pp. 267–269) has a brief description of how Philip Knight started Nike.

163 **Reaching the peak of athletic excellence**. For research on the experiences of athletes who have reached the top of their sport, see Gould, Jackson, and Finch (1993), and Jackson, Dover, and Mayocchi (1998).

bibliography

Bandura, A. (1977). Self-efficacy: Toward a unifying theory of behavior change. *Psychological Review, 8*, 191–215.

Brewer, B.W., Van Raalte, J.L., and Linder, D.E. (1993). Athletic identity: Hercules' muscle or Achilles' heel? *International Journal of Sport Psychology, 24*, 237–254.

Cooper, A. (1998). *Playing in the zone: Exploring the spiritual dimensions of sports.* Boston: Shambhala.

Csikszentmihalyi, M. (1975). *Beyond boredom and anxiety.* San Francisco: Jossey-Bass.

Csikszentmihalyi, M. (1990). *Flow: The psychology of optimal experience.* New York: Harper & Row.

Csikszentmihalyi, M. (1993). *The evolving self.* New York: Harper Collins.

Csikszentmihalyi, M. (1996). *Creativity: Flow and the psychology of discovery and invention.* New York: Harper Collins.

Csikszentmihalyi, M. (1997). *Finding flow: The psychology of engagement with everyday life.* New York: Harper Collins.

Csikszentmihalyi, M., and Bennett, S. (1971). An exploratory model of play. *American Anthropologist, 73*, 45–58.

Csikszentmihalyi, M., and Csikszentmihalyi, I. (Eds.) (1988). *Optimal experience: Psychological studies of flow in consciousness.* Cambridge: Cambridge University Press.

Csikszentmihalyi, M., and Larson, R. (1986). *Being adolescent.* New York: Basic Books.

Csikszentmihalyi, M., and Larson, R. (1987). Validity and reliability of the Experience Sampling Method. *Journal of Nervous and Mental Disease, 175*, 526–36.

Csikszentmihalyi, M., Rathunde, K., and Whalen, S. (1993). *Talented teenagers: The roots of success and failure.* New York: Cambridge University Press.

Deci, E.L., and Ryan, R.M. (1985). *Intrinsic motivation and self-determination in human behavior.* New York: Plenum Press.

Dryden, K. (1989). *The game: A thoughtful and provocative look at life in hockey.* Toronto: Harper & Collins.

Duda, J.L. (1992). Motivation in sport settings: A goal perspective approach. In G.C. Roberts (Ed.), *Motivation in sport and exercise* (pp. 57–92). Champaign, IL: Human Kinetics.

Ferguson, H. (1986). *The Edge.* Cleveland: Howard E. Ferguson.

Gould, D. (1998). Goal setting for peak performance. In J.M. Williams (Ed.), *Applied sport psychology: Personal growth to peak performance* (3rd ed.) (pp. 182–196). Mountain View, CA: Mayfield.

Gould, D., Jackson, S.A., and Finch, L.M. (1993). Life at the top: The experiences of U.S. national champion figure skaters. *The Sport Psychologist, 7 (4),* 354–374.

Hanin, Y.L. (1995). Individual zones of optimal functioning (IZOF) model: An idiographic approach to performance anxiety. In K. Henschen and W. Straub (Eds.), *Sport psychology: An analysis of athlete behavior* (pp. 103–119). Longmeadow, MA: Mouvement Publications.

Inglehart, R. (1990). *Culture shift in advanced industrial society.* Princeton, NJ: Princeton University Press.

Jackson, P. (1995). *Sacred hoops.* New York: Hyperion.

Jackson, S.A. (1992a). Athletes in flow: A qualitative investigation of flow states in elite figure skaters. *Journal of Applied Sport Psychology, 4 (2),* 161–180.

Jackson, S.A. (1992b). Elite athletes in flow: The psychology of optimal sport experience. Unpubl. doctoral dissertation, University of North Carolina at Greensboro.

Jackson, S.A. (1995). Factors influencing the occurrence of flow in elite athletes. *Journal of Applied Sport Psychology, 7 (2),* 135–163.

Jackson, S.A. (1996). Toward a conceptual understanding of the flow experience in elite athletes. *Research Quarterly for Exercise and Sport, 67 (1),* 76–90.

Jackson, S.A., Dover, J., and Mayocchi, L.M. (1998). Life after winning gold I: Experiences of Australian Olympic gold-medallists. *The Sport Psychologist, 12,* 119–136.

Jackson, S.A., Kimiecik, J.C., Ford, S., and Marsh, H.W. (1998). Psychological correlates of flow in sport. *Journal of Sport and Exercise Psychology, 20,* 358–378.

Jackson, S.A., and Roberts, G.C. (1992). Positive performance states of athletes: Toward a conceptual understanding of peak performance. *The Sport Psychologist, 6 (2),* 156–171.

Jones, G., and Hardy, L. (1990). *Stress and performance in sport.* Wiley: Chichester.

Kelly, J. R. (1982). *Leisure.* Englewood-Cliffs, NJ: Prentice-Hall.

Knox-Johnston, R. (1969). *A world of my own.* London: Cassell.

Krakauer, J. (1997). *Into thin air.* New York: Random House.

MacAloon, J. (1981) *This great symbol.* Chicago: University of Chicago Press.

Maslow, A. (1968). *Toward a psychology of being* (2nd ed.). New York: van Nostrand Reinhold.

McInman, A., and Grove, R. (1991). Peak moments in sport: A literature review. *Quest, 43,* 333–351.

Murphy, S. (1996). *The achievement zone: 8 skills for winning all the time from the playing field to the boardroom.* New York: Putnam.
Murphy, S., and White, R.A. (1995). *In the zone: Transcendent experience in sports.* New York: Penguin.
Myers, D.G. (1992). *The pursuit of happiness.* New York: Morrow.
Myers, D., and Diener, E. (1995). Who is happy? *Psychological Science, 6,* 10–19.
Nideffer, R.M. (1989). *Attention control training for sport.* Los Gatos, CA: Enhanced Performance Services.
Orlick, T. (1986a). *Psyching for sport.* Champaign, IL: Human Kinetics.
Orlick, T. (1986b). *Coaches' training manual to psyching for sport.* Champaign, IL: Human Kinetics.
Panorama (1998). Towards 2000: Donovan Bailey, Sprinter. *Panorama.* Ansett Australia in-flight magazine, May 1998, p.136. Sydney, NSW: POL Corporate Publications.
Parducci, A. (1995). *Happiness, pleasure, and judgment.* Mahwah, NJ: Laurence Erlbaum.
Randolph, M. (1997). On the edge. *Outdoor Canada,* May, 1997, pp. 24–28, 51–54.
Ravizza, K. (1998). Increasing awareness for sport performance. In J.M. Williams (Ed.), *Applied sport psychology: Personal growth to peak performance* (3rd ed.) (pp. 171–181). Mountain View, CA: Mayfield.
Silver, A.D. (1985). *Entrepreneurial Megabucks.* New York: John Wiley & Sons.
Sun, W. (1987). *Flow and Yu: Comparison of Csikszentmihalyi's theory and Chuang-tzu's philosophy.* Paper presented at the meetings of the Anthropological Association for the Study of Play. Montreal, Canada, March, 1978.
Taylor, P. (1996). The trade. *Sports Illustrated, 84 (9),* 33–39.
Thompson, J. (1993). *Positive Coaching.* Dubuque, IA: Brown & Benchmark.
Veroff, J., Douvan, E., and Kulka, R.A. (1981). *The inner American.* New York: Basic Books.
Veenhoven, R. (1988). The utility of happiness. *Social Indicators Research, 20,* 333–354.
Weiss, M.R., and Chaumeton, N. (1992). Motivational orientations in sport. In T.S. Horn (Ed.), *Advances in sport psychology* (pp. 61–99). Champaign, IL: Human Kinetics.
Williams, J.M., ed. (1998). *Applied sport psychology: Personal growth to peak performance.* (3rd ed.). Mountain View, CA: Mayfield.
Yukelson, D. (1998). Communicating effectively. In J.M. Williams (Ed.), *Applied sport psychology: Personal growth to peak performance* (3rd ed.) (pp. 142-157). Mountain View, CA: Mayfield.
Zinsser, N., Bunker, L., and Williams, J.M. (1998). Cognitive techniques for building confidence and improving performance. In J.M. Williams (Ed.), *Applied sport psychology: Personal growth to peak performance.* (3rd ed.). (pp. 270-295). Mountain View, CA: Mayfield.

index

about the authors

Susan A. Jackson and **Mihaly Csikszentmihalyi** combine their backgrounds to present the most authoritative work on the phenomenon of flow in sports, bringing together the expertise of the world's leading authority on flow with the leading researcher in the sports field.

Stephan Riek

Susan Jackson, PhD, won two awards for her doctoral research, which examined the flow experience in elite athletes. Jackson has continued to conduct research and publish articles on flow in sports, and is known internationally for her work on the subject.

She brings to her work the perspectives of athlete, coach, teacher, sport psychology consultant, and university lecturer. Jackson lives in Brisbane, Australia, and lectures in the School of Human Movement Studies at Queensland University of Technology.

Christopher Csikszentmihalyi

Mihaly Csikszentmihalyi, PhD, developed the concept of flow in the mid-1970s and has pioneered research on the subject in work, social, and educational settings ever since. His early research on flow explored play and happiness and involved a number of prominent athletes. He has published 10 books, among them the ground-breaking *Flow: The Psychology of Optimal Experience,* as well as *Creativity: Flow and the Psychology of Discovery and Invention* and *Finding Flow: The Psychology of Engagement With Everyday Life.*

Csikszentmihalyi is an elected fellow of the American Academy of Arts and Sciences (1997) and the Hungarian Academy of Sciences (1998). He is the C.S. and D.J. Davidson Professor of Management at Claremont Graduate University in Claremont, California.

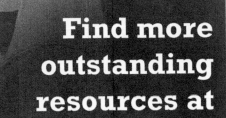